M000043817

Pulled by the Heart

A woman's real-life story of living and
escaping the Middle East

Pat,

thank you for
today and

hope you enjoy!

Mary J. Wolf

2011

Pulled by the Heart

A woman's real-life story of living
and escaping the Middle East

Nancy T. Wall

DeForest Press
Rogers, Minnesota

PULLED BY THE HEART. Copyright © 2009 by Nancy T. Wall. All rights reserved. No part of this book may be reproduced in any form whatsoever, by photography or xerography or by any other means, by broadcast or transmission, by translation into any kind of language, nor by recording electronically or otherwise, without permission in writing from the author, except by a reviewer, who may quote brief passages in critical articles or reviews.

ISBN-13: 978-1-930374-28-7
ISBN-10: 1-930374-28-3

Author's photo and photos on pages 48, 54, 68 and 168 by MC Kinney, Appleton. All other photos property of Nancy T. Wall.

Cover design by Nancy T. Wall and Linda Walters, Optima Graphics

Printed in the United States of America

First Printing: June 2009

Published by
DeForest Press
PO Box 383
Rogers, MN 55374
763.428.2997   1.877.747.3123
www.deforestpress.com
Shane Groth, Publisher
Richard DeForest Erickson, Founder

Library of Congress Cataloging-in-Publication Data

Wall, Nancy, T., 1950-
  Pulled by the heart : a woman's real-life story of living and escaping the Middle East / by Nancy T. Wall.
    p. cm.
  ISBN 978-1-930374-28-7
  1. Wall, Nancy, T., 1950- 2. Americans--Middle East--Biography. 3. Women--Middle East--Biography. 4.   Intercultural communication--Middle East--Case studies. 5. Culture conflict--Middle East--Case studies. 6. Escapes--Middle East--Case studies. 7. Intercountry marriage--United States--Case studies. 8. Intercountry marriage--Lebanon--Case studies. 9. Islam--Social aspects--Middle East--History--20th century 10.   Middle East--Social life and customs--20th century. I. Title.
  DS61.52.W356A3 2009
  306.84'5092--dc22
  [B]
                                            2009015421

For my children, Nadine and Manar

If not for them,
this story would be much different …

Contents

Preface

Someone once wrote, "Stories have to be told or they die, and when they die, we can't remember who we are or why we're here." I'm writing this story for my children, so that they will remember who I am, and so that I might remember who I was, and so that the part of me that died years ago might once again begin to live.

Books have a life of their own. They do not start as words, but as inklings, thoughts, trying to surface from their subconscious prison. I'd had such inklings for many years. Then in the summer of 2003, a number of events occurred that told me it was time for my thoughts to take shape on the written page. First, I had foot surgery that required me to be homebound, which put a stop to my whirl-wind of activities and meant I suddenly had time on my hands. Second, my mother gave me a box and said, "I thought it was time you have these. This box has every letter and postcard you ever wrote us from the Middle East."

I caught my breath, stunned. There they were, in the original blue airmail envelopes, each postmarked date sharing a time I had lived long ago and had tried so hard to forget. I placed them carefully, almost reverently, on the corner of my kitchen table. They sat there for two weeks before I had the courage to sit down and read through them. For reading them meant remembering and in a larger sense, reliving a time more than twenty years earlier. It was time. Time indeed.

I've been encouraged throughout the years to write this story. First by Ellen Kort, Wisconsin's first Poet Laureate, whom I had the privilege to work with in an advertising agency shortly after arriving back in the States. Then by my daughter, whose request was always on my mind. And more recently, by my son. It's for them I now share my story.

Acknowledgments

Thank you to Linda Walters at Optima Graphics for the continual encouragement and downright determination and passion to make me do it right.

Thank you to my new friends, Shane Groth and Dick Erickson of DeForest Press, for believing in the story and believing I could do it. Mostly, thank you for allowing my book to be true and unchanged and trusting that hope, peace and connectedness between the two cultures could be honored and respected with the publication of this book.

Thank you to my mother and father, Gloria and Harold Thurner. Without my mother's gift to save and cherish the past and both of their strong sense of family, the letters would have been lost and much of the detail with it. Thank you to the rest of my family and friends for their enthusiasm, fervor and support.

Lastly, thank you to my husband, Duncan — without his steadfast support and love, this book would never have become a reality.

Prologue

He had a light complexion and deep brown eyes — a dead give-away he was from Syria.

At least it was a dead give-away if you grew up in the Middle East and caught his accent. But since this was Milwaukee and I was raised in the small city of Neenah, Wisconsin, the only thing I knew for sure when I first saw him was that I was in love.

It was 1970 and I was 19 years old. As the oldest of six children, I had left the security of my family to attend Prospect Hall, an all-girls school in Milwaukee. I walked into the Open House at the Milwaukee School of Engineering (MSOE) on April 4 with a couple of my girlfriends, decked out in a purple mini-skirt, matching purple V-top with a purple suede, beaded vest, large hooped earrings and pink, patent leather platform shoes. We were attending the Foreign Students' Night and there he was — a tall, slender man with dark, long curly hair standing at a table against the wall at the back of the room. He stood out among the students: well-groomed, foreign and aristocratic. He smiled. I was intrigued and in love from the beginning.

His name was Maher and we dated from that moment on. He had such a different air about him and was so handsome that when he came to my apartment to pick me up, my roommates and friends would either stay or stop by before he arrived just to see him. He also drove a new, orange-red Camaro.

Maher graduated from the Milwaukee School of Engineering in 1972. His parents attended the graduation, traveling from Beirut, Lebanon. They were not pleased to see him involved with an American woman and were determined to take him home to marry someone of their own choosing.

1

They did take him home to Beirut and the night he came to say goodbye was the first difficult night of my young life. I believe it was for him, too. When he left my tiny apartment and I closed the door, I placed my hand and head on the door and wept silently. It was as though I could feel his hand on the other side as I heard him weep. It was the first time I had ever heard a grown man cry. And then he was gone. It was over. After being with him for two years I thought I would never see him again.

Maher's parents were, however, unable to convince their son to forget me. He continued to call me from Beirut. We had talked about marriage before he left, but for his parents it would be a scandal for him to marry a Christian. They simply could not consent to such a thing.

Maher got a job as an industrial accountant for a large American accounting firm in Beirut. We didn't see each other for 18 months. Finally, Maher insisted to his family that he wanted to see me and was sending for me to come and visit. I had no idea at the time what that took and how he did it, but he did. I was working for a law firm in Milwaukee as a legal secretary and took a week vacation during Christmas of 1973 to join him. As it turned out, I called my office from Beirut and extended my vacation for another week.

I did not stay at Maher's home while I was there. Instead, he rented a small flat for us. It was my mission to prove to Maher's family that I wasn't going to take their son away from them to America. And I guess I needed to know for myself if this relationship could work half a world away from my own family. His parents were cordial but the objections remained.

I was very fond of the city of Beirut but knew I had to go back home. A year passed and though I was still very much in love with Maher, I decided I needed to get on with my life. I figured a new career would help. I had always wanted to work for the State Department and decided to take the necessary tests. I wrote Maher and told him that my papers would be in order soon and that I was willing to go anywhere the State Department sent me. Two months later, he flew to Milwaukee and proposed.

I left for Beirut, Lebanon, in April of 1975 to be married, five years from the time I had first met Maher. I was 24 years old and he was 29. My parents were surprisingly supportive. Perhaps because I had known Maher for five years; perhaps because he was always very kind and thoughtful; perhaps because they could see how much in love I was with him and he with me. Cultural and religious differences were never discussed. Maher had lived here for a number of years, was not a practicing Muslim, was well educated and came from a wealthy family. All seemed well. Of course, I'm sure they were not happy to see me leave the States, but they had always allowed their children to make up their own minds and they knew how determined I was.

Chapter One

Surprises in Beirut

I'm nervous and anxious as the plane descends into the Beirut Airport in April 1975. The moment I've been waiting for — to marry the man I love in this city in Lebanon where all my dreams will come true. I assess my appearance carefully. After such a long flight, I try to straighten my skirt and blouse, and yes, the corsage my mother pinned on me at the airport in Appleton, Wisconsin. It is still alive, though slightly wilted, a reminder of what I have left behind. I touch it lovingly. I add a little fresh lipstick, comb my short blonde hair and smile into the pocket purse mirror. I'm ready.

As the plane nears the runway, I hear what sounds like explosions. That can't be. I look out my window. The plane is still intact and I can't see anything that would explain the loud booming noises. Another explosion? We land. There is commotion.

Suddenly I realize there is fighting close by, right next to the runway.

Maher and his father are there to meet me as I deplane and quickly take me away. I try to take in the sights and smells of this new country that I had seen only briefly a year ago — my first impressions now of a country that will be my home. It is a beautiful sunny day. White and red flowers are all around, as are the palm trees. The air is sweet with the smell of flowers, the air pleasant. Paradise — until I see the men with machine guns. There are roadblocks with soldiers gathered in small groups talking and whispering.

Maher and his father want to make sure I am safe. They must be fearful, but I am unaware of any danger. Little did I know a civil war would be in full swing in another month.

Beirut is densely populated. The "homes" are what we would consider apartments or condos in the United States. Because of space, they build up instead of out. There are no individual homes on separate pieces of property.

The homes in Beirut could be rented or owned. The Tarabishis owned a home on the top floor of a building. There was a "concierge" who opened the door for us. As we exited the elevator and walked into the Tarabishi home it was like walking into a whole new world. Shiny marble floors went as far as I could see. As Maher led me past the great room or "salon," the first thing I noticed was a thick, massive Chinese carpet almost as large as the room itself. Shades of turquoise, beige and pink in the carpet highlighted large, gold furniture — covered with real gold — and tapestries on the oval backs with similar colors. Traditional Syrian inlaid pearl furniture was also scattered in the huge room along with the largest porcelain vases I had ever seen. Hanging on the high ceiling above was a huge chandelier. When

I asked Maher how they got it in the home, he said they had to use a crane through the balcony.

In the Middle East, men are named after their first-born son. Since Maher's older brother, Nouman, was the first-born son, their father's name was Abu Nouman, which literally means, "father of Nouman." The women are also named after their first-born son, so Maher's mother was Umm Nouman, or sometimes we called her "Madame." Umm Nouman literally means "mother of Nouman."

I shared a room with Umm Nouman, my future mother-in-law. (Talk about getting to know the in-laws quickly.) I could not determine her age. She had the blackest of hair and dark skin — darker than any of her children. She was of Spanish/Arab descent. Since Maher was 29 and Umm Nouman's eldest child, a daughter Nadia, was 10 years older than me, I determined she must be 55 to 59 years old. She was about 5' 3" and a bit chubby. She never wore makeup, other than a little lipstick if she was going out and was always frowning. I couldn't determine if she was just thinking or disturbed about something. When she was angry, she was the scariest person I had ever known. I decided she was the one I had to please. When she smiled, though, it was a beautiful smile. Her dark, black eyes sparkled as if a white light was in the center.

The Tarabishis had a maid who had been with the family since the children were young. Her name was Umm Saad. Her dark hair was worn pulled back tight into a bun at the nape of her neck. Her deep brown-black eyes showed life only when made to smile. Her dark skin accented deep creases on the sides of her mouth. She could not have been more than 5' 2" tall. She kept her head and eyes slightly down whenever I was near or anyone came to visit. I wondered if she was just shy, but then realized this was part of the culture. She was Egyptian and her family was still in

Egypt. I knew only that she must have a son since her name was Umm Saad. It was amazing how someone so small could do so much work in a rather large house. Not only did she do all the cleaning but she was also an excellent cook.

The first thing every morning, Umm Nouman would light a cigarette and Umm Saad would make her coffee. Umm Nouman was a chain smoker. I learned that her father had the first cigarette factory in the Middle East and she came from money. I guess that's why she ignored her husband if he irritated her. Abu Nouman was tough in his own way and occasionally I would hear him scold her. She would say something, then simply walk away. This, in the Middle East, where women were supposed to be subservient. I'm sure it was because of her family's money and stature.

Umm Nouman would sit with her legs crossed, smoke her cigarette and sip her coffee in the smaller parlor room — never in the salon or formal dining or living areas. She would just stare out and I would wonder what she was thinking about. She never read anything while enjoying her coffee and cigarette. It was as though this was one of her favorite things to do — just sit quietly, in peace by herself. I never dared to disturb her.

Though I never drank coffee before, I was anxiously anticipating my very first cup, never mind that it was Turkish! I was asked how I liked it. Not really knowing, I said, *"Biddon sikkur"* (Without sugar). I was learning the language (not reading or writing) as quickly as possible and learned just as quickly that Turkish coffee without sugar was intolerable — at least for me. Without making a face, which is not polite in the Arab world, I realized I was going to die if I didn't remedy the situation. I quickly changed my mind and asked for *sikkur*. I came to love Turkish coffee this way and began to visit the kitchen every day to order it, but let both Umm Saad and Umm Nouman know that I wanted to learn how to make my own *ah way* (coffee).

Though it sounds easy, making Turkish coffee is an art — it isn't simply dumping coffee into a pot, turning it on and walking away. First you have to determine how many cups of coffee you want to serve. Unlike the huge mugs of coffee we guzzle down in the States, Turkish coffee is served in very small cups, about three to four ounces in size, and is sipped. It is very strong — like a double-shot of espresso with an extra two shots thrown in for good measure. Once you know how many cups you'd like to serve, you add heaping spoons of coffee and sugar into the Turkish coffee pot and heat it on the stove. The trick is to keep it from boiling over, which I found was much more difficult than it sounded. It took a lot of practice and careful, patient watching before I could make it correctly.

Little by little, Umm Nouman and Umm Saad taught me how to make coffee and to cook Arabic meals. It was fascinating to watch them prepare the food without measuring cups or spoons and no recipes to follow. Everything was done by sight, smell and taste. It was intimidating at first, but I learned to love to cook this way. Enormous meals were prepared from a very tiny kitchen, even in the most sumptuous of homes.

It was clear as I watched these two women of very different means work and respond to each other, that their relationship had been bound together through the years. Though Umm Nouman would seem to scowl at Umm Saad at times, every once in awhile I would see the affection between them. Open affection between the older adults of the family was not evident. I felt Umm Saad was overworked, but I knew she was very much a part of the Tarabishi family and that they loved her. I, too, grew to love her and still think of her to this day.

In the beginning weeks after my arrival, it occurred to me that even sleeping was a different experience here in Beirut. Every day at sunrise, I was awakened by the *Allah u Akbar* (the call to prayer) from the mosque. The chanting over the loudspeaker was loud enough to be heard throughout the city. I eventually learned to sleep through this Muslim call to prayer — another sign that I was growing accustomed to living here.

Even though the letters I wrote home to my parents indicated Maher's family liked me and indeed welcomed me, I felt I was being watched for the slightest mistake. Remember, I was not the ideal candidate for their son. They only accepted me because Maher had insisted I was the only one he would marry. The family was obviously very wealthy and I was not. I tried hard to be so good and do everything right — and I didn't even know what that was. I soon discovered that Maher's sisters never washed their own hair, never did their own nails or manicures or pedicures. They never even shaved their own legs — a woman came to wax them. How amazed I was. I would sneak away and do my own nails.

I remember being in a room closed off by large, sliding wood doors. One of Maher's sisters was on the other side, talking to someone about what a peasant I was coming from a small city in the States. I even did my own nails! She spoke in English and I wondered if she was doing this on purpose. She had to have known I was on the other side of those sliding doors. I was shocked to hear her talk about me in this manner. I froze and stopped breathing, then continued to do my nails quietly.

Maher had warned me that his sisters were beautiful and perfect and that I needed to be the same. So I tried very hard to be as perfect as I could and ignore what they said. I hoped that in time they would come to accept me.

Afternoon coffee (Turkish) was a common custom and neighborhood ladies were always invited — women only. They wore fashionable modern clothes and were always greeted warmly with kisses and the welcome phrase I could now say: *"Ahalan wa sahlan."* This day the women were all from our building and Umm Nouman escorted them to the room where we were having coffee. I was already seated but got up to be respectful, smiled shyly and didn't know exactly what to do. I waited until they were seated and then sat down.

I must have been an object of curiosity for them. I have no idea what they thought of me since they did not speak English and only Arabic was spoken. It was clear in their glances toward me that they didn't mind checking out this American, though it appeared they were fine with me being there. Every opportunity I had I smiled back. I was lost in their conversation trying to figure out what they were talking about. They talked so fast I could only catch a word here or there.

I slowly became more involved in these afternoon coffees as I learned a few words, but mostly I sipped and smiled and listened. Listened because Arabic women are so full of expression! Their voices swooped and swooned. I could only imagine what gossip they were talking about. It was very exciting and I was glad to be part of it. None of these women, however, became friends, since eventually all would flee the building to safer areas because of the war.

I remember one day when one of the women was all of a sudden very sad and almost in tears. Later, when they were gone, I asked Umm Nouman through Maher what made the woman so sad. She said that because of all the shooting and danger in the city, she had become so nervous that she had miscarried. She said she knew many who this had happened to.

The fighting in the streets was unreal to me. I didn't understand the politics of this. It appeared that no one in the Tarabishi family was political either. They just wanted peace. Who was doing the fighting? It seemed as though enemies changed daily.

Maher was working for an accounting firm called Saba Company. He went to work when the fighting wasn't too bad. I wanted to work as well but there were obstacles, especially since I didn't speak Arabic well enough yet. I needed to find a business that dealt with English-speaking clients, I figured. Looking for work as a woman wasn't an issue; many women in Beirut worked. But for now I would have to spend my days at home.

I passed the time playing *towley* (backgammon) with Umm Nouman on a board made with beautiful mosaic inlaid pearl from Syria. We also played *qatours* (cards). I was playing cards with her one day and I caught her cheating. Since I was learning everything new here I observed as much as I could — no matter how small the detail. So, of course, I was watching her intently, not trying to stare and noticed she slipped a card out of her hand and tried to replace it with another. I couldn't help but laugh and she knew I caught her. She laughed too. What a breakthrough! From that moment on she would teach me Arabic words. She spoke no English. When an airplane flew overhead, she would point and say *tierra*. I would repeat the word until it was pronounced correctly then she would nod her head in approval. I was feeling better about sharing their home and their beautiful country. I was falling in love with Beirut, the food, the people and the customs.

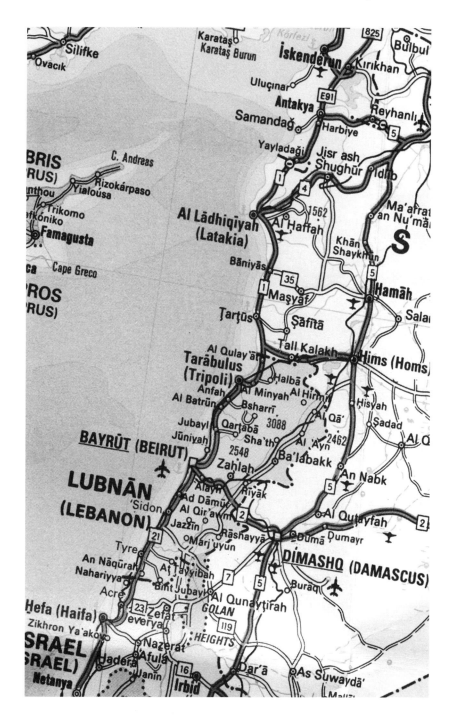

Chapter Two

Paris of the Middle East

Beirut was called "the Paris of the Middle East." I learned later it was so much more than Paris. You could feel the love in this city. For the first time in my life, I saw men holding hands with other men and women holding hands with other women as friends — because they were close friends. They offered one another three kisses on the cheek in greeting — one on the right, one on the left and another on the right. Everyone called their friends, acquaintances and strangers *habeebte* or *habeebe* (my love), depending if you were female or male. When someone entered your home, you said *"Ahalan wa sahlan,"* which meant "Welcome." And once they entered your home, they could not use anything of their own. For example, not their own cigarettes, but those of the home they were visiting — usually in a large bowl in the center of the table in the receiving room. And if it was close to mealtime, visitors were always invited to stay for that meal. I found this culture irresistible for its friendliness and hospitality.

Outdoor *souks* (markets) were plentiful in Beirut. Abu Nouman, Maher's father, was the "fruit picker" in the family. Well-bred and well-dressed, he always wore a dress shirt and pants or suit. He held his head high and walked with a very straight back. He was not very tall, perhaps 5'8" or 5'9". His hair was white with a little wave on top, which he brushed back. He spoke French and prided himself on his limited vocabulary of English — it was a godsend to me that I could get my message through to him by speaking half English and half Arabic. He caught on quickly and I learned from him as well, especially when it came to fruit. He was exceptional when it came to picking *bitek* (watermelon), mangoes, muskmelon and other fruits. He never made a mistake. So, I would go with him and watch and learn. Every piece was chosen carefully. It was first by sight and then by feel and lastly by smell — never touching the fruit except with his hands. He would carefully replace inferior fruit and when he found the right one, would hand it to me so I could see, feel and smell the difference. I became a very good "fruit picker" with Abu Nouman's help.

At the main meal, which was mid-day (between 1 p.m. and 2 p.m.), fruit was always the last part of the dinner, with large platters served. You could hear everyone's delight in the selection of the fruit of that day. It was at these meals that I learned how to properly peel a mango (or any fruit) with very little mess. The trick is to cut a small circle around the top of the fruit, where it was connected with the plant, and remove it. You then slide the knife under the remaining peel and make 4-5 slices downward equally spaced around the fruit. This makes little sections you easily pull away from the fruit one at a time, especially if the fruit is ripe. I also learned how to dispose of olive pits while eating — properly. (Did I mention I was from a small city in Wisconsin?) Simply fork the olive into your mouth. When you're done chewing, close your hand into a fist with the thumb and forefinger face up. Silently eject the olive pit into the small hole your closed fist provides and place it on your plate.

The indoor and outdoor cafés were bountiful on Hamra Street, the most popular street for restaurants in Beirut. They were totally different from the American cafés or restaurants I had been to. A variety of hors d'oeuvres (as Americans would call it) arrived before ordering the main dish. I had no idea what I was eating at first and tried everything put in front of me. Textures were varied from smooth *hummus* to the crunchy *fatoush* with toasted bread pieces in it. Everything was an adventure to me and I found the food delicious — so delicious that I should have limited my intake at first. My stomach did not react well to all the different Arabic foods, especially *blu khe ah*, a chicken dish. I remember spending several days staying home and running to the bathroom during my "transition" from American food to Arabic food.

Speaking of the bathroom, I had never seen a bidet before. I remember the first time I used the main bathroom thinking how different everything was here. Next to the toilet was something I had never seen, like the lower half of a toilet with faucet handles. I thought I would carefully turn it on and see what happened. Up came a spurt of water that scared me. Wasn't the water supposed to go the other way? Thankfully, I had turned it on partially and not fully. "Hmmm," I thought. "I'll have to ask Maher what this is for." I walked out and privately asked him about it. He laughed. Apparently and truly, I was an unworldly and untraveled woman.

He explained it to me. I knew I would never use that thing.

By the time we married, I was down to 107 pounds (48 kilos), still trying to keep the food down. Once I stabilized, however, I was up to my normal 118 pounds (53 kilos). I remember Abu Nouman saying, "I'll have to put some pounds on this girl!" It seemed he liked women with some meat on them — hence Umm Nouman, I thought to myself with a smile.

All nationalities of restaurants from Lebanese to Portuguese were represented in Beirut. They loved going out to eat and experiencing a variety of foods. The waiters (always men) were extremely well-trained and appeared to love what they did for a living. I noticed that every restaurant we went to seemed to have the highest of standards for food and service.

Nightclubs were busy and never seemed to close. The Lebanese loved to have a great time, to party and dance. I remember sitting down and immediately being served an array of nuts and other niceties before our drinks even arrived. Everyone wore the latest fashions from Paris and Italy. The people were genuine and friendly to me and tried to speak English for my sake. It was a wonderful life until the gun bursts clattered — then the city shut down, section by section.

Beirut was very modern, very fashionable and very "hip." Hence its nickname "the Paris of the Middle East." I couldn't figure out how a waiter could be so well dressed on a waiter's salary. In fact, it appeared everyone dressed well and was well mannered. I began to see that it was part of their culture — they indeed felt themselves very civilized and cultured in the ways of fashion, entertainment and cuisine. They felt they had the best of everything. Their money was spent on looking good. But I would learn there were other parts of the society that did not fare as well.

One day we went for a drive with Maher at the wheel. Umm

Nouman (I never saw her drive a car) wanted me to see something, though I had no idea what it was. We stopped at a Palestinian camp. I had never seen anything that looked so depressing and poor. She kept saying as she pointed, "Look." I believe it was the only word she knew in English. It didn't seem dangerous to drive here — there were no road blocks — and while she showed me the camp, she did not let on how she felt about it. I remained silent and looked. Makeshift walls from whatever material could be found were covered with large pieces of aluminum as roofs. The floor was dirt and there appeared to be no electricity or running water. I was too shocked to even ask a question. No one spoke.

Chapter Three

Fighting in the Streets

It was the end of May 1975, and I had been in the house for two straight weeks because of the gunfire. I had never heard a gun go off before arriving in Beirut and at first the *pop pop pop* sounded like small firecrackers in the distance. By this time, however, having been in Beirut for over a month, I had heard thousands of rounds of ammunition, along with bombs and explosions, which occasionally landed close enough to feel. It was impossible for us to prepare for a wedding. We couldn't get out. On every corner there were mounds of sandbags with men and guns and children with machine guns.

Then on June 1, we were able to leave the house, but only during the day. We felt it was safe to travel to Hamra Street — the street of cafés and stores located in an area always considered safe from the trouble spots. I remember Maher driving the family Buick there. (Maher's father had purchased six Buick cars from the States and imported them into Beirut. He sold five and kept one for the family.) We had almost arrived when I looked out the passenger side and saw an open jeep with young men and boys, each with a machine gun. The one nearest me, a mere 13 or 14 years old, looked at me.

Unfortunately, I looked him in the eye. He slowly raised the machine gun from his lap and pointed it directly at me. I heard Maher's voice say, very calmly, "Turn your head slowly and look straight ahead. Then don't move." I did just that and we continued down the street. They did not stop us. I couldn't help but think that my blond hair announced to the world I was an American. We continued to Hamra Street and a favorite café. I needed a drink, something strong — like Turkish coffee.

The roadblocks were something we avoided at all costs. Roadblocks meant danger in the area. If they stopped you and didn't let you pass, there was a good chance you'd be held — perhaps never to be heard from again. We definitely avoided them that day.

During the last week of May the fighting was fierce and right outside our building, the building owned by the Tarabishis. From our top-floor home, the day was pretty typical for living in a civil war: no one went to work because of the danger, no going out of the home because of the shooting. Indoor chores were performed, including washing down the balcony floors and watering the plants, which were abundant. Abu Nouman loved his plants and would water them before Umm Saad washed the floors. Instead of using a mop, Umm Saad used a bucket filled with water and a large gray cloth. With both arms down on the ground, she'd sway back and forth with the cloth to clean the floors. It was labor intensive but very effective. Water was always the choice for cleaning floors — not sweeping. Even outside of the homes, you would see vendors and merchants every morning washing the entrance of the store and sidewalk. It was always very clean.

Maher was playing backgammon (he was a very good player) with his mother and I was watching. The front balcony was wide open and all of a sudden shooting broke out that sounded much too close. Maher grabbed me and pushed me to the floor. We crawled on hands and knees to the hallway where it was safe, away from the windows and balconies. We sat there until all the shooting stopped, which seemed a very long time. For some reason, I was not frightened. Perhaps because I had not lived through what everyone else had in this country, or perhaps because everyone else was so worried about me, or simply because I did not understand the danger. However, I did realize how much I had taken my freedom for granted in the States, and I missed that precious freedom.

Chapter Four

Immersed in the Muslim Culture

There was a break in the violence and on June 2, 1975, I began my first job for the Far East Travel Agency. I was wild with excitement. The other employees were all Lebanese — I was the only foreigner. They hired me because they had English-speaking clients. Though they spoke English, it was broken, but not bad. It was a perfect fit for me. They were very kind and I loved working there from the beginning. Finally, I had a job, which was important for two reasons. First, it showed that I was more than an outsider or visitor in this country — I could make a positive contribution to my new homeland. Second, I could start contributing financially to our goal of getting our own place after the wedding. "Flats" as they called them, were very expensive in Beirut and it would take my salary in addition to Maher's to be able to afford one.

I was greeted and introduced to everyone. We all worked in one large rectangular room except for the boss who had a separate office. My desk had a typewriter, a phone and everything else I needed. The telex machine was on another desk close by. One side of the office fronted the main street and was all windows, so it was very light and cheery. Everyone in the beginning just stared at me, but soon everything fell into place and I felt very comfortable, especially when I could help by talking to an English-speaking client over the phone. These clients were delighted to speak with an American.

On June 19, I became a Muslim. In Lebanon at that time, there were no "mixed" marriages allowed. You were either both Christian or both Muslim. In order to marry the man I loved, I needed to become Muslim. I knew my parents would understand even though they were Roman Catholic and raised me in the Catholic Church. They believed it didn't matter what you called your God, as long as you believed in Him. I would not become a "practicing" Muslim — just in name — though I would follow and respect its customs.

I accompanied Maher and his father to the Muslim "court" where I met three sheiks. Sheiks were the religious leaders of the Muslim faith, like priests in the Catholic Church. I presented my papers, including passport, and a document I had obtained from the American Embassy. It declared that I was of the Christian faith and that there was no reason why I should not be permitted to marry Maher, a Syrian. It also stated that I had not previously been married. Maher presented his passport and his birth certificate. I had to repeat and acknowledge that I understood an oath, the testimony of faith, *ash-shahada*, which I was required to say in Arabic: *"Ashhadu anna la ilaha illa Allah, wa anna Muhammadun rasoolu Allah"* (I declare there is no God but Allah, and

Muhammad is His messenger). Then an official document was drawn up and I was registered as a Muslim. The whole process took no more than an hour.

Maher's father then met with another sheik and set a date for him to come to the house and perform our wedding cere-mony. The time and date was set for Saturday, June 21, at 4 p.m.

On the day of the wedding, I awoke at 5:30 a.m. — everyone else was sleeping. I was anxious to get up but stayed in bed until 7:30 a.m. so that I did not disturb anyone. Maher had some things to do in town and Nadia, his eldest sister, had to go to work.

Maher had given me a pre-wedding gift — a bottle of the most expensive perfume you could buy — Joy. I was so excited that I dropped it and it broke. I was horrified. I couldn't believe I did that! But Nadia was right there. She immediately grabbed some tissues and said, "You have to make use of this wonderful perfume." I watched as she dabbed the Joy perfume from the floor then said I should put it in my shoes! How clever, I thought. When I told Maher he simply smiled and said it was okay — not to worry. Nadia was right.

I polished my blue high heels and ironed my blue silk wed-ding dress, Maher's shirt and the silk tan suit I was going to wear the next day. I had at least established myself in the house so that I could do my own ironing. It took me a long time to convince Umm Saad that I could and wanted to do this. I felt it necessary to show I was useful in some small way, that I was raised to do my own work. She would never let me do anything, not even make my own bed. I wondered if this was a tug-of-war between two cultures, where I was supposed to take care of myself in America and she was supposed to take care of me here in Lebanon. Or perhaps it was simply a tug-of-war with my own self-esteem, that I wanted to prove I could contribute something, even if it was simply ironing. Yet something else pulled at my heart — a desire to lend a helping hand to Umm Saad with her heavy workload — but perhaps that wasn't my place either.

Maher had ordered the cake (since I had no idea where to get it or what to order) and carried it in about 1:30 p.m. It was two layers high, all white and decorated with white hearts and white-coated almond candies; and topped with a bride and groom with a heart shape over them. In many ways it was similar to a wedding cake in the States, except for the almond candies. (Candied almonds, along with those in pastel colors, were an expensive treat and very popular in Beirut.) A silver tray of white and blue almond candies sat nearby. Everything matched very nicely. Maher had a tailor-made light blue suit with a tailor-made white shirt with a dark tie. My dress was a darker shade of blue.

My parents

I had sent a telegram to my parents in Neenah informing them of the date and time of our wedding at the Tarabishi home. It was 2:00 p.m. and I was hoping to hear from them by phone. (While I took phones for granted, Maher told me it took them two years to get a phone in Beirut. It wasn't just putting in an order, either. If you didn't know someone or pay someone a lot of money, you didn't get a phone. That's how things worked here in the Middle East.) The phone rang in the foyer and I ran for it, wedding dress and all. It was my mom, dad and family. I knew all would be well this day ...

After talking to my family, I called Madame (Maher's mother) to our bedroom and motioned her with my hand to sit next to me on the bed. I put my right arm around her and told her in Arabic that I loved Maher very much and that I was going to be the best wife I could be to him. She understood my broken Arabic. With tears in her eyes she said that she now had three daughters: Nadia, Ruby and Nancy. I had so hoped for that. I kissed her and she told me to call her Mother now, instead of Madame.

Maher went to pick up the sheik and returned at 4:15 p.m. I walked into the salon where the sheik, Maher, Maher's parents, Nadia, Aby and Tony were sitting. Aby and Tony were my witnesses. Aby was a male friend of Maher's who had come back to Beirut with Maher from the States. Tony was once Maher's roommate in Milwaukee. That was it. Women were not allowed at the ceremony except for family. I remember thinking this wasn't right and had an uneasy feeling about it, but I dismissed it as just a plain, awful fact of life. I was determined to learn and accept the customs of the Muslim faith, little by little.

At first I was disappointed that there was no formality about the wedding — so simple, too simple, I thought. I had no real wedding dress and it bothered me, which was surprising. I thought it really didn't matter, but it did. And, funny thing, I wanted a white wedding dress, too. But it wouldn't be proper since the ceremony was so informal and in the home. I finally realized this and settled for the simple blue silk dress. It was a short-sleeved, one-piece silk dress that crossed over at the waist (tying on the inside at the opposite side of the waist) and snapped at the other side. It was three-quarter in length and it didn't take long before I fell in love with it. It was perfect, just like the entire day. I carried a single red rose into the room.

Everyone stood as I entered. Then we all sat down and I was introduced to the sheik. He proceeded to tell Tony about the

Abu Nouman and the sheik
in the Tarabishi home

Muslim faith as it relates to marriage. Tony then translated and made sure I understood and approved of everything he was saying. In the Muslim faith the man is to provide everything for his wife, she is not responsible for anything, nor does she have to do anything in the way of earning money. The man is totally and completely responsible for his wife in all respects. A symbolic amount of money is acknowledged as being received now, before the wedding, after the wedding another sum of money is supposed to be paid to the bride. This is for divorce purposes, since nothing is given to the wife at the time a divorce is granted (if it is granted at all). Traditionally, a woman can ask for anything she desires at this time. Any amount of money, a camel — anything she desires. Funny, I had never been in the position before to get anything I desired. My parents had never asked me that. My teachers had never asked me that. Come to think of it, no one had ever asked me that question before now. What was it I really desired? I think they were scared to death I was going to ask for a lot of money, so they suggested a small token amount of 10 sterling pounds (about $15). I remember thinking I was a modern woman and 10 pounds was okay because it was just symbolic, so I agreed. How young and naïve I was.

The sheik then asked me, "Do you take Maher as your husband for 10 sterling pounds?" I said "Yes," and that was that. We were man and wife.

The sheik said *"Mabrook"* (Congratulations) and everyone kissed us in the European fashion — both cheeks. Nadia cried, even Maher's mother had tears in her eyes. After Maher and I finished receiving everyone's kisses, we faced each other. The sheik pointed out in Arabic that we kissed everyone but each other. So we kissed each other in the European way (both cheeks) and everyone laughed.

Umm Nouman and I had grown closer by my wedding day

We exchanged wedding rings while pictures were being taken. My ring was actually three gold bands fused together. The two outside bands were one of white and one of rose gold, with the middle band yellow gold. Maher's ring was white gold and

Finally we were able to wed

matched perfectly to the white gold band on my ring. We had them engraved with the date of our wedding on the inside. Maher also gave me another ring. It was the white gold ring with the large yellow diamond that I had worn briefly in the States before Maher left for Beirut after graduation. His mother had given it to him. That day he gave it to me.

We cut the wedding cake, which was served with ice cream. The long table for seating was beautiful. The red linen tablecloth with gold thread design had matching red napkins, silver candelabras, red candles and sterling silver plates and silverware on top. It was absolutely lovely and it was much more than I expected. Red and white roses and carnations were everywhere. I had prepared nothing myself. Maher, Umm Nouman and Umm Saad had done everything.

At the end of the ceremony, Maher and I signed a marriage document. We were married at 4:30 p.m. and within an hour we were on our way to our honeymoon night in the mountains of Lebanon.

We drove to Beit Eddine, an hour and a half away. It was a

Hotel in Beit Eddine

village high in the mountains and we stayed at the hotel that was formerly the castle of King Amir. The castle was so grand and breathtaking, I truly thought I was dreaming. It had been built in the thirteenth century and renovated now as a hotel. There were 22 suites in this enormous castle and our suite was the largest I had ever seen. It featured high, arched stone ceilings, huge oriental rugs, oriental dressers and a long, beautifully carved wooden sitting desk. Our bedroom had a king-sized bed and a bathroom of marble with every modern convenience (even my favorite, a bidet). It was a combination of the very old with the very new. Off the bedroom was a back door, which led to a huge rounded terrace with a large water fountain in the middle. I was overwhelmed with the wealth and beauty of the castle. From our suite we could walk down a long, narrow flight of curving stairs to the swimming area and another huge terrace.

The carpet at the bottom of the pool

A small archway of deep purple bougainvillea graced three private tables that over-

The bougainvillea

looked the pool, each table set close to the edge of the mountain. Looking down from our table, you could see the magnificent rectangular pool that included an exquisite Oriental rug of bright reds and blues — at the bottom of the pool! It extended from one end to the other and was beautiful, extravagant and surprising, all at the same time. To the left, I could see all of Beirut below with the Mediterranean Sea hugging the city's shoreline. The two famous rocks, called the Pigeon Rocks, jutted up from the water just off the beach. Gazing to my right were the world-renowned cedars of Lebanon, showing off their rich, vibrant coats of green on the hillside of the mountains.

I had never seen anything this magnificent. The colors were the most vivid I had ever seen — the deep blue of the Mediterranean Sea, the deep green of the cedars, the deep purple of the bougainvillea. Surely there was no grander place on earth. Surely I could never be happier than at this moment in my life — in my new homeland.

We walked to the cavernous dining room for dinner. The ceiling was so high I couldn't estimate its enormous arch. The table was the length of the room and could seat over a hundred people. There were large, antique ornate candelabras set at intervals on the table. We sat at one end nearest the entry. I felt like we were in an old Roman movie. Fresh exquisite bouquets of flowers filled the room, each in an enormous beautifully decorated urn. We drank wine out of our sterling silver cups, a wedding present from my sister, Debbie. That evening after dinner, an expensive, complimentary French bottle of champagne was delivered to our room.

We drove back to Beirut Sunday night and were welcomed with kisses, hugs and flowers from friends and family. After spending some time with family, we retired to our room. Our bed had beautiful light-blue sheets with a flower design and a bouquet of flowers had been placed between our pillows. In fact, the whole room was adorned with flowers. But the most important gesture was a note Maher's father had printed in English on a piece of paper, "Happy Marriage."

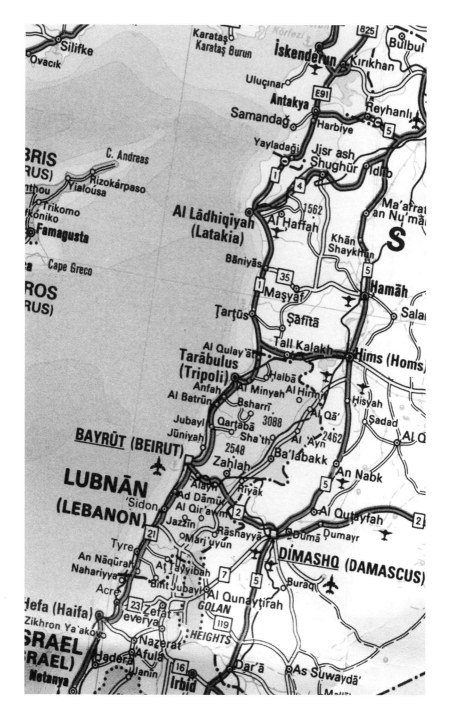

Chapter Five

Moving Targets

*I*t was early September 1975, and the war was heating up with even more violence. In addition to the bombs and machine gun fire, we heard there were many snipers. One evening I headed down to the kitchen for a bit of pistachio *halawa*, an Arabic breakfast food of pistachios, sugar and ground sesame seeds that I loved. It seemed I could never get enough of it without looking like a glutton, so I would sneak into the kitchen when I thought no one was looking, get a knife and carefully lift out a piece from the round container — not too big because then someone would notice — but just enough to satisfy my sweet tooth. As I turned on the kitchen light, a bullet ripped through a small, open window at the end of the kitchen only 8 to 10 feet from me. I dropped to the floor, gathered my wits, then quickly jumped up to turn out the light. I went down to the floor again as fast as I could. I had no idea if I was a target because I was an American or if someone was just shooting to kill another innocent victim. Or perhaps it was just someone who loved *halawa* more than I did.

The afternoon coffees with the women grew even more stressful now, yet it was the only outlet for these women to talk to each other and share their feelings. I watched their faces and listened to the stories of how more women were miscarrying because the bombings were making them so nervous. Then, one by one, families began leaving the building, moving temporarily to safer areas.

Growing up in America, the Civil War between the North and the South wasn't much more than a history lesson for me. With Beirut now in a full-blown civil war, that history lesson became much more real and dangerous. The fighting in Beirut that broke out in early September between Muslim and Christian suburbs was now in our neighborhood. In fact, our building was on the border of the demarcation line and No Man's Land.

After the first day of fighting, Maher's family (except Nadia) left for Damascus, Syria, where they had a home. Nadia stayed because of her job. Maher and I stayed, determined not to give up.

Each day the fighting became worse. Buildings near us were riddled with bullet holes. Somehow our building remained intact. We heard of people being hit by snipers and people found dead. We never had to witness this, thank goodness. I could only compare it on a very small scale to the Battle of Gettysburg; but here you couldn't see the enemy. Instead, they were hidden amongst the buildings. Soon Nadia could not travel safely home from work, for fear of being shot, so she stayed with a friend in a safer area. So for a week, Maher and I were alone. We did not dare take one step out of our home. We only moved from our bedroom to the hallway, like moving from one bunker to another, because they were the only safe places. The rest of the home was an invitation to a sniper's bullet. The large, open balconies made for easy targets. It was strange to think that people you didn't know waited outside with the sole intent to kill you. Day after day, night after night, it got worse.

By now everyone else in the building had fled. We were truly alone. We thought we could survive and that the fighting would soon stop — that there would be peace. But there was no peace. No quiet — day or night. Like a bad song on the radio that plays over and over, we listened to the whine and explosion of rockets, the deadly chatter of machine gun fire and the *pop pop pop* of small arms. We listened and waited. Listened for how close the sound was and waited for the explosion and the damage and to see if we had been hit when the split-second silence followed. It shook my insides, but I never let it show. I knew that the last thing my new husband needed was a hysterical wife. He never showed he was scared either, though I knew he had to be.

Why did we stay? It has been said that the sanest reaction to an insane situation is insanity. On the one hand it made absolutely no sense to stay when the time between life and death was measured in seconds. And yet, the nightmare of war and death and destruction and evil and hatred was so overwhelming that anything normal, no matter how small, was the only lifeline to survival. That is why people went to work and stayed in their homes and woke up each morning wondering if they would be alive the next morning — to prove in some small way that life and goodness still remained in the world.

I went to the bathroom one morning and when I sat down, I felt a sudden whoosh of massive blood and clots. I

Beirut bombing

must have miscarried — I didn't even know for sure that I was pregnant. I told no one. Since I had not even mentioned the possibility of being pregnant to Maher, I did not tell him either.

Fighting escalated day by day until one morning the concierge of the building, who was still working, came to us and informed us that heavily armed *Faydayeen* (Palestinian guerillas) had taken over the building. They were setting up rocket launchers on the roof — on our roof. I'll never forget the look on Maher's face. We were really a target now. If people started shooting out of our building or from the rooftop in defense, we would receive the same gunfire in return. Our building now would be a target and destruction would follow.

It was also very difficult now to get out of our building because of the roadblocks in place. Maher would be able to leave because he was Muslim living in a Muslim area, but I was a big problem. Because of the Israeli-Egyptian Agreement brokered by America, citizens of the United States were not well liked, my blonde hair and fair looks made me an easily-identifiable target. Everyone feared that if I were seen, my life would be in danger.

One day when we were in desperate need of basic food, I wrapped my hair completely up and went downstairs. Nadia was back with us at this time but was too scared to accompany me. I smiled shyly at the men with guns in our lobby, said *"Sabah el khair"* (Good morning) and went quickly on my way. At the store, I spoke only Arabic as well. With just a few words I purchased bread, sugar and a few other items we needed. As I reached our building, I heard that a very young boy was missing and I asked the concierge what happened to him. He had just been killed by gunfire. I quickly entered our building and headed up to the top floor.

The destruction of both human lives and to Beirut in general was appalling. Why was this going on? What was being accomplished? While the news called it a civil war, I heard different answers ranging from the Syrians, the Palestine issue, the Lebanese government, and more. Perhaps that is why I took chances and did things that I really should not have done. I didn't think it was real at times. It made no sense.

What did make sense was that we needed to get out. Nadia had connections to the Palestinian fighters through a friend. She arranged to have an armed fighter (we were told he was the bodyguard to one of the top PLO leaders) take us out. I remember clearly the hard firm knocks on the door. I stood behind Maher while he opened the door. There stood the largest Palestinian I had ever seen. He was not tall but very wide and looked very strong. Under each arm he carried a machine gun. I stepped back. He must have been told about me since he was not surprised to see an American, or the money was good enough for him that it did not matter. He asked if there was anything in a safe that we wanted to take and Maher said no. I was almost certain the safe contained several large precious stones along with Umm Nouman's 10-carat diamond, but we did not know this man and he could have easily taken what he wanted. All bets would have been off in terms of our safety. I was glad I remained silent.

From the conversation going on between the men, everything

seemed okay. We packed a few things and left. Riding down the elevator, I was amazed at how much room this man took with his machine guns. I wondered what we were getting into and what could happen if we chanced into the wrong people. He stood in front of us seemingly ready for anything.

Once downstairs in the open lobby, we were quickly ushered into a very small Fiat. I remember thinking there was no way the bodyguard was going to fit. Small cars were everywhere in Beirut and were essential since the population was so dense with so little space for parking. I slipped in the back seat behind the bodyguard, who had packed himself in the front with one machine gun on his lap and one next to him between the seats. We sped off as though shot out of a cannon, zigzagging down streets to avoid gunfire and rockets, never going in a straight line for very long. We reached a safe part of the city near Hamra and stayed for ten days, the three of us in a furnished flat. After the ten days, we took a taxi back home to the Tarabishi building. It was safe again — for a while.

At the beginning of October things seemed better. Then,

An apartment building near us in Beirut

in the middle of October, things heated up again. There were many kidnappings. Two Americans were kidnapped one block from our building with no further word about them. Maher would not let me out of his sight for fear of me being kidnapped. We had not been able to go to work for a week. My office closed because of the critical economic situation, and I lost my job.

At first I was crushed. There

went our dreams of being in our own home for Christmas. It meant so much to me at the time. I couldn't bear the thought of spending Christmas with Maher's family, with no Christmas tree or any other tradition I had grown up with. I had intended to celebrate just like we had in the States, in my own home. Somehow that would make life feel more normal, even in a war-torn city like Beirut.

The American Embassy issued an evacuation to all American citizens. Not just once, but twice. They even called me. I declined. My parents called me as well. When their call finally got through to me, bombs were going off in the background and I was trying to hide it from them. When they asked about the noise I said it was nothing, making up excuses as fast as I could. Though I desperately wanted to talk with them, I had to get off the phone before the bombs gave me away as a liar. I knew my parents must be crazy with worry, but I would not leave my husband.

My life was with
my husband

Chapter Six

Sand Dunes, Camels
and a Five-Star Hotel

Two families returned to the building in November 1975. This was a relief to us. But it was still impossible to leave the house. There were snipers everywhere. And no one knew when the fighting would erupt. The streets of Beirut were completely deserted. There was no movement at all except for those fighting.

I tried hard to understand this war. I heard it was a class struggle — the poor against the rich. The poor peasant Muslims fighting the rich Christians. The Palestine Liberation Organization (PLO) entered the scene, fighting for the poor and oppressed. But fighting for what? The government was corrupt, apparently. There were no housing programs, no hospitalization or healthcare programs and no social security. So unless you were rich, you had no means to any social services. As a young woman from the

United States, it was hard to comprehend. There was no middle class here. Of course there was much more going on, but this was all I knew at the time. My husband's family was Syrian, not Lebanese. The Syrians were also trying to take control of Lebanon. But these things were never discussed in front of me. To me it appeared that the Syrians loved Lebanon and they too wanted peace.

Our home and building, so far, were still intact. We had not been broken into, robbed or burned like so many others near us. Another cease-fire was called. We again were stuck at home, but we never gave up that the situation would change and things would return to normal. We had each other. We were very much in love and Maher kept my spirits up — especially when he could tell I was missing home.

Then something happened that changed our lives. The company Maher worked for wanted to send him to the United Arab Emirates in the Arabian Gulf (also known as the Persian Gulf). He worked as a consulting engineer for them and had been working for one of their clients, Marblo. The company's general manager and owner lived in Beirut where they had a factory. But there were two more factories, one in Sharjah and one in Abu Dhabi. Maher was requested to travel to the Gulf to consult and organize these two factories. With the war on, Maher refused to leave me behind by myself as his parents were still in Syria, and I refused to go to Syria without my husband. To my surprise and delight, Maher was given the okay for me to accompany him.

On November 14, Maher and I left for Dubai in the United Arab Emirates. I wondered what was ahead in this strange land of sand dunes, camels and Bedouins.

We arrived at the airport in Dubai. This was so different from Beirut. The airport was very small and there seemed to be nothing except desert in sight. Modern conveniences were really new to the area — even having an airport. We were taken to a small, local Arab hotel in Sharjah, a small neighboring emirate. I didn't know what I expected but it was very rudimentary. I guess the fact that there was a hotel at all was amazing. I found out that there were two hotels, this one and the Sharjah Carlton, which was right on the Arabian (Persian) Gulf waters. The Sharjah Carlton was the premiere hotel in the Gulf at the time, but we could not get a reservation — even with the general manager's considerable influence. We were able to get in the next day.

Well, this was my first experience with down and dirty in the Middle East. Thankfully it was November and it was not hot — it was only in the 80s. We opened the door to our room and the look on Maher's face said it all. I can't remember which of us was more horrified. I believe it was my husband. A small twin-sized bed was covered with dingy-colored sheets and a thin, red blanket filled with holes. There appeared to be another small room to the right, so I slowly walked over and stood in the doorway. It was a small bathroom that contained an open shower in the corner and a toilet on the other side. I looked up at the ancient showerhead and turned it on. A trickle of water came out. But what really caught my attention was the added attraction of the biggest cockroaches I had ever seen, crawling near the showerhead and the tub drain. I stifled a scream and pulled myself together thinking, "It could be worse — we could be out in the desert in a tent." But in truth, this was worse. Maher and I knew there was nowhere to go or nothing we could do, so we lay on top of the red blanket and prayed the night would pass quickly.

The next morning we anxiously waited outside the hotel for our driver from Marblo to take us to the Sharjah Carlton. It was a short ride in the desert and I saw a modern, four-story building that looked very nice from the outside. As we walked into the lobby, it was very clean and modern. I was ecstatic. I could see ahead that there was a large dining area with floor to ceiling glass doors and on the other side was the beach and the Gulf waters. I could hardly contain myself. Not only was the beach and sea gorgeous, but to the left, a few steps up, was a large rectangular pool surrounded with chairs. Now I was in heaven. There were no other buildings nearby, nothing but beach on either side of the hotel. My own private paradise.

I didn't wish to waste a single minute so I encouraged Maher to proceed to our room, which I found quite simple but clean and attractive. Maher needed to go to the Marblo office and factory; we knew I would be quite safe here. I changed into a swimsuit and threw on a good swimsuit cover. (By good cover I mean something that went from my shoulders to knees and was not see-through.) It

UAE Dirhams

was time for me to explore this place.

I remembered that outside the lobby to the left was a shop through which you could get to the pool. I was confident that I could communicate with people and said to myself, "Here we go!" Everyone I encountered seemed to be delighted with this blue-eyed, fair-skinned woman who was trying to awkwardly speak their language. They were very kind to me. I could see they sold Arabian trinkets and other miscellaneous items. I'd return with *dirhams* to purchase things later but right now the pool was calling.

Once outside, I walked up a couple of stairs to the pool and was handed a towel. I continued straight-ahead and then around to the left, where I selected a chair at the corner of the pool closest to the sea. This would be the same chair I occupied every morning. The beauty unfolded in front of me over and over, and I wondered how a small city girl from Wisconsin got here. The Gulf was a

Sharjah Carlton

deep-blue fantasy, the sky cloudless and perfectly light blue. I laid down and let the warm sun sink into me, breathing deeply in and slowly out, completely content.

The Marblo staff was having lunch at the Sharjah Carlton, as we did on many occasions. The owner, his wife, secretary and many others were also staying at the Sharjah Carlton. We became a family in many ways. I remember feeling very relaxed here with no anticipation of bombs going off or snipers to worry about. We all sat at a long table. I was at the end closest to the clear, glass doors going out to the beach. As usual, we enjoyed the excellent Arabic food of *hummus, tabouleh*, grape leaves, *khubz* (Arabic bread) and a *mezza* of other items. We were talking, laughing and just enjoying the day when a huge boom sounded nearby. The room went still. I immediately dropped to the floor and covered my head. When no other noises followed, I looked up and saw that I was the only one on the floor and everyone was looking at me. As it turned out, someone going out to the beach didn't see the closed glass doors and walked right into them. I felt so foolish and looked into Maher's eyes. It was the first time I really knew what a toll the war had taken on me. I slowly got up, laughing lightly at my folly and resumed eating lunch. I couldn't help but think that in a few short weeks, when Maher's consulting job ended, we would be returning to Beirut.

Chapter Seven

*Damascus — Joy, Intrigue
and Disappointment*

Two days and it would be Christmas 1975 — my first away from my family in the States. I lay in the Arabian hot sun dreaming of fluttering snowflakes and banks of snow. When I awoke, I walked to the beach from the pool and lazily kicked the warm water by the shoreline. Suddenly something bit me. I ran out of the water only to discover what looked like two sharks close to the beach. Everyone else had noticed these two large fish and had stayed out of the water. Obviously there were dangers I was not aware of and I would be more careful in the future.

Maher came back to the hotel one day with a sparkle in his eye, a smile on his face; I could see his excitement. Marblo offered him a job as Production Manager at the new factory in Sharjah. What a welcome surprise. It certainly solved our dilemma about going back to Beirut. Maher, however, was very concerned about me living here in the desert in an all-Muslim country. This would be much different than living in Beirut, where the city was very cosmopolitan and the weather more mild. He wanted to make sure I would be happy.

I told myself I would go anywhere on earth with my husband. Besides, Sharjah in the Arabian (Persian) Gulf wasn't so bad. In fact, I was rather fond of it already. It was a decision that once made, however, there would be no turning back; no being unhappy. We would have to throw our hearts into the new situation completely. In terms of Maher's career, it gave him room to grow and put to use his industrial engineering degree. We would also finally have our own home and be independent of his family. There were so many things to consider — it was nice Marblo gave him some time to think about it.

Christmas Day came and we left the Gulf for Damascus, Syria, to spend a month or two with Maher's mother and father. We would make our decision there.

Damascus, Syria — what a place on this earth. It was so completely different than Lebanon. There were not many modern conveniences here. Even the Tarabishi home was old, though they were prosperous. They lived very simply here. The whole trip was a surprise to me. I did not expect to see such barrenness in the land or fewer modern conveniences then they had in Beirut. I did not expect to see a stripped down version of the Tarabishi home in Beirut. Everything was cold, dark and dreary — the weather and the house. The heat didn't seem to be on even though there were old radiators. The bathroom did have a shower, which surprised me given what I had seen of the rest of the house. However, the next day when I used it, it was literally a dribble. It took me a very long time to wash my longer hair and

I was afraid the water would end before I was done. Outside, everything looked barren. The poor looked to me to be very poor and there were so many. I had never seen such mass poverty. I was struck by the fact that no one smiled. So unlike Beirut, Lebanon or the Gulf.

I'll never forget the Damascus *souk* (market). It was grand in its size with very high, arched ceilings. It was so old; I had no idea what it was made of. Old men with turbans and deep crevices on their faces indulged in one of the Middle Eastern's favorite pastimes — sucking on *hookahs*. These long, brass water pipes with glass bases were ornately decorated and scattered everywhere. The smell of hashish was prevalent even in the large quarters, spread by the hustle and bustle of so many people. The smell of spices was heavy yet pleasant. Women covered in their black *chadors* with gold jewelry and delicately designed red henna hands and feet moved gracefully about, shopping. I marveled at this sensory overload — there was just too much to take in with so many local people walking and milling around. I did notice that there weren't any foreigners, however.

We came upon a store with beautiful fabrics of all kinds. I could see the name Tarabishi written in Arabic above the entrance. As Abu Nouman escorted me in, it dawned on me that this really was the Tarabishi store I had heard about. It was a large store — larger than most near it. Everything was very neat and tidy, as I would expect from Abu Nouman, who was meticulous in his appearance and everything he did. A variety of fabrics, not of only every kind but of every color, graced the store. Abu Nouman showed me the beautiful fabrics and picked some tan silk fabric out for me. He also gave me two exquisite covers, what we would call dusters in America, one blue and one turquoise, made of sheer material with real gold threads. (These I still have

Real gold threads

and wear when I travel abroad.) He was proud of these fine fabrics, especially the ones with real gold threads, and even said in English, "Real gold threads." I was honored and said, *"Shu kran ik teer"* (Thank you very much).

This is where Maher and his father's family originated — where their roots were — in Syria. The store was a part of their heritage, of who they were. A small piece of the larger Syria represented in this marketplace that was beautiful and fascinating. But it wasn't all glitter and gold. You could easily get lost in this *souk* and instinctively I felt it could be a very dangerous place for a foreigner. I stayed close to Maher and Abu Nouman.

I learned that Maher's father had owned theaters and vast amounts of land, among other things, here in Syria. The government confiscated it all a long time ago when Nasser took over and nationalized the country. Private individuals lost their holdings to the government. Abu Nouman, perhaps anticipating what was going to happen, buried a lot of gold bars to protect his wealth. He then smuggled the gold bullion out of Syria to Lebanon and started over again.

I was told that Maher's grandfather, apparently a very handsome man with blue eyes, rode a white stallion. What a dashing sight that must have been. In the Middle East, if you saw a light-skinned Arab with blue eyes, they were probably Syrian.

While still on our visit to Damascus, I was having pain in my mouth. Strange, since I had such excellent teeth. Maher took me to the best dentist in Syria. As I entered his office and looked around I thought, "If this is the best, what are the rest like?" The room was no more than 10' x 10' and cluttered. The dentist chair looked like it was the first ever made. It was high backed with black leather, covered with cracks and well-worn. I didn't see an X-ray machine.

I was introduced to him and he motioned for me to sit down in the chair. He looked into my mouth and said that my wisdom teeth had to come out. Of course, he didn't speak a word of English, but I got the gist of it. You might think I would have been a little bit curious about how he was going to take out my wisdom teeth since everything looked so primitive. But I just went along with it, feeling that everything would be all right. My husband was certainly confident that everything would be fine. So, out they came.

When he was done, the dentist stuffed the holes with cotton and showed me the teeth he had just pulled. They were hooked at the roots. Oh dear, I thought. I hoped the bleeding would stop. We went to a small bar that was very dark and Maher encouraged me to drink until I could feel nothing. I did.

Another cold, dreary day in Damascus. Only on this day, Maher's mother accused me of stealing something. I couldn't understand what she thought I stole but she was so angry, it frightened me. Something was terribly wrong. She was yelling and screaming.

Maher told me what it was — some old wire hangers from her closet were missing. Hangers? I was devastated. She was insane to accuse me of something so trivial. How could she think I would take something from her room, or that I would even enter her room without being invited? Had I somehow changed from a beloved daughter-in-law to a foreign thief?

In the commotion, I left the home through the front door without anyone noticing. I was so upset I needed to get some air and think. That was not a very wise thing to do in a country like Syria. I had no passport on me — no identification at all. But I was too upset to think clearly. Eventually I came to a large round-about, where enormous steps led up to a small peak. I walked up the steps and sat at the top, looking all around me. No one was around and apparently no one had seen me. I didn't have any idea what I was going to do. Maybe just stay here until dark. I still knew where I was in relation to the Tarabishi home, but it was probably not a good idea for me to go any further. Oddly enough, I wasn't in a panic but remained very calm. I sat with my elbows on my knees and my hands on my face.

Soon, looking down, I saw my husband and his father walking the streets calling out my name. Maher seemed frantic. I just sat there and watched. Perhaps moving to Sharjah would be a good idea after all. Finally and reluctantly I called out to my husband. I wanted him and his father to know how hurt I was and that it was not a good idea to be so cruel to me. I waited, sitting there until my husband came up to me. We returned to the Tarabishi home. Nothing was ever mentioned about that incident later on, and I was never accused of stealing anything ever again.

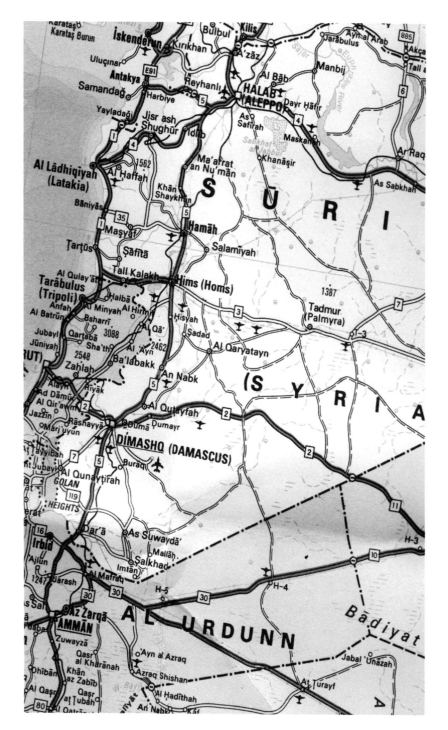

Chapter Eight

Home Is Where the Head Is

On January 24, 1976, we left Damascus and arrived in Sharjah, via Dubai, for good. Maher and I had agreed that he should accept the job. I was excited to begin this new life in our new home and was sure I would love it. The company had already rented a new flat with two bedrooms, and we would be able to order our furniture right away. The company paid for everything.

The United Arab Emirates (UAE) is actually seven emirates or sheikhdoms on the Arabian (Persian) Gulf and the Gulf of Oman. The UAE, as it is commonly known, consists of Abu Dhabi, Ajman, Dubai, Fujairah, Ras al-Khaimah, Sharjah and Umm al-Qaiwain. Abu Dhabi is the largest emirate territorially and the capital of the UAE. During our stay, the ruler of Abu Dhabi was the president of the federation. Dubai is the port city

Dhow building, an ancient art

in the UAE and the hub of commercial activity. Everyone traveled to Dubai for the entertainment and restaurants. Sharjah, our new home, was the third largest city in the UAE. These emirates were all British protectorates until the United Arab Emirates was formed in 1971, and Britain announced they were leaving. Apparently there were a lot of feuds and wars between the rulers of the emirates in the past. The smaller emirates seemed largely dependent on the larger emirates.

The old and new merged in the UAE. The time-honored tradition of building *dhows* (boats) was beautiful and extraordinary. You could still see them building *dhows* of wood by hand near the edge of the water. Jewelry, especially necklaces, of gold or silver boats was very popular for those living in the Gulf. The Gold *Souk* (Market) was something to behold. I had never seen so much gold — not even in the movies. The gold was sold by weight and then by intricacy of the work. It was all at least 18 karat gold. Local women, completely covered in black *chadors* along with covered faces, showed off arms and necks lined with gold bangles and necklaces as they casually shopped.

Though oil was discovered in the 1960s, boatbuilding, fishing and diving for pearls were the staples of the region. Dates were also grown in Umm al-Qaiwain. As oil was discovered and produced in several of the emirates, it became the ultimate source of their wealth.

A dramatic increase in building was going on in the Gulf. The area attracted many nationalities and more English was being spoken, though Arabic was the language of the country. Sharjah was becoming a mecca for banks, which lined the main street. The roads were still sand but construction was everywhere.

Grocery stores were hard to find in the Middle East, but joy of joys, they had one in Sharjah. It wasn't much bigger than our bathroom growing up in Neenah, barely 6' x 10', but oh, it was a treasure! The store was called Spinneys and had items from the States and Europe that came by boat. It was a precious moment to find a product from the United States. If I was lucky enough to see a familiar product, I'd carefully reach for it, like a fragile, precious package, and put it in my basket of "finds." Because items took three to six months to clear the port and arrive at Spinneys, I'd be so disappointed if I opened a package and found it moldy or full of bugs. I loved that little store. It was like treasure hunting every time a new shipment came in. I was a regular customer and everyone got to know me. Funny, but it wasn't until I lived here in the Gulf that I learned to appreciate what I had left behind in the States.

The greeting customs here in the Gulf were different, even from those in Beirut. My husband and I still used the three kisses to the cheeks in greeting someone we knew, followed by *"Salam alaykum"* (Peace be with you) and *"Keyf halak"* (How are you). I noticed now that sometimes the local men touched or kissed noses as a greeting. Maher said that sometimes noses substituted for cheeks, but the greeting was always a way to show respect to elders or one who had authority.

In the Arab world, heads of state demonstrated brotherly ties between their nations by embracing and kissing one another's cheeks. When two friends met on the street, it was not uncommon to see them joyously express their affection by kissing on the cheeks, though to outsiders it looked rather over-the-top. But it was perfectly common and accepted in the Arab world, whose people, in general, shared more enthusiasm in their relationships. Arab men driving along in cars would suddenly stop — it didn't matter if there was traffic or not — and get out of their cars to greet a friend and start a conversation. Darndest thing I had ever seen.

More and more I came to realize how important it was to pay attention to the culture I lived in, especially here. The Arabs liked to take their time; they enjoyed a leisurely pace. It was a mistake to rush them. If you were in a business meeting and started to feel things slowly dragging on and happened to glance at your watch or refuse to take the time to drink their Turkish coffee before discussing business, the meeting was over. It was an insult to rush them. It was like saying, "You are not important enough to take so much of my time," or "I don't like the way you do things." To the Arabs, time was a precious gift, something you shared with a friend. I began to understand how important the little things were. The tone of your voice. Averting your eyes, in humility. Smiling. Trying to speak the language, no matter how little you knew. Not only was it important culturally, it was important for me as a person. Like Americans, the Arabs love their culture and land and wish for others to respect that.

I was delighted to see some furniture stores opening in the Gulf, especially since I now had the chance to decorate our home. I picked beige shag carpeting for the foyer, living and dining rooms and dark brown carpet for the bedrooms. A cognac (rusty-brown) couch with matching chairs went in the living room, along with an oval, black marble table for six (made to order from Marblo) with six chrome chairs covered with soft, black leather. It was a start. I even bought goldfish, a sure sign I was here to stay.

I was, for the first time, a housewife. I loved my new home, though it was a lot of work keeping up with the sand that continually seeped through the windows. I began experimenting with Arabian cooking, remembering what I had learned from Umm

Nouman and Umm Saad, both great teachers and great cooks.

I did not, however, love the cockroaches. They were everywhere. One day I was walking in the foyer and suddenly froze as I saw a monstrous cockroach on the wall directly across

Our "flat"

from me. It was at least 4" long and big enough, I swear, to eat the goldfish I just bought. But it wasn't just sitting there; it was looking at me. Staring me down as though I were its next meal. I couldn't decide whether I should run, hide or attack. The cockroach, however, didn't have the same problem with indecision. It leapt from the wall and flew at me, closing in fast like a small dive-bomber. I was so startled, then outraged by the gall of this hard-shelled intruder trying to take over my house, that instead of screaming I ran for a shoe. I didn't stop to think about who the cockroach was in a former life, either. Needless to say, I won that battle, though I'm not sure I ever wore that shoe again.

There were bigger things as well. As I lay in bed one night, I heard a tiny *click click click* sound above my head, like the toenails of a dog on a wooden floor. A rat ran across the headboard. I made sure that only happened once. The owner of the building began fumigating for rats and cockroaches after that on a regular basis. The rats never returned. I wish I could say the same for the cockroaches.

The people of the Gulf dressed traditionally. Women wore a long black *chador* with veils to keep their eyes covered. The men, unlike in Beirut, wore a long white *dishdash* (dress).

One day while walking down the street with my husband, I saw a local Arab, whom I assumed was a poor Bedouin. He seemed very old, with dark skin and deeply etched wrinkles on his face. He wore a red and white headdress, carried a wooden staff in his hand, and around his waist toward the middle front hung a large dagger in its sheath. He was barefoot and dusty. "You see that man?" Maher said to me. "He's one of the richest men in the country." I never assumed anything about anyone from that time on. Things are not always as they seem, especially in the Middle East.

Many people from India and Pakistan lived here. In fact, they were the largest foreign population in the Gulf. Cows were sacred, so they too roamed untouched. Sometimes a donkey with its owner would be in the road. The old with the new, surrounded by construction growing all around. I felt like a pioneer at times in an Old West town that suddenly made way for the railroad. Dusty old roads springing up with shiny new buildings, food and fashion merging from around the world, people walking or riding donkeys sharing the byways with automobiles. Like a vision in a glass orb, it was a picture of where people had been for hundreds of years and a quick glimpse of where they might be in the future. Literally a crossroads of time, space and technology. I felt honored, and overwhelmed, to be sharing a small piece of that sacred space.

There were restaurants and nightclubs in the few hotels in the Gulf. The hotels were the only places allowed a liquor license. You could buy liquor for yourself in limited amounts if you lived in Sharjah and applied for a permit. Since Muslims are not allowed to drink, I got a permit on my American passport because it did not state a religion, as Maher's did. Almost everyone drank liquor in the younger generation, those in their twenties and thirties, but certainly not in public. To do so would be a disgrace. In fact, anyone caught drinking in public would be taken immediately to prison. I never saw Maher's parents drink. One of the stories everyone heard was that occasionally a custom's official from the port in Dubai would call a member of the royal family to tell him he needed to come down immediately and get his container because it was "leaking."

Foreign women were allowed to drive in the United Arab Emirates, so I got my license right away. One day as I was driving there was a traffic jam, which I couldn't figure out since there was not much traffic yet in Sharjah. No one was moving, so I got out of my car and walked over to where the commotion was taking place to see what was going on. Two local Arabs were arguing and had stopped their cars in the middle of the road so no one could get by. I was walking past one of the cars and saw a machine gun on the floor in the back seat. Another Arab was standing by the car, probably the owner. I looked at him; he looked sternly back at me since he knew I saw the gun. I smiled shyly, then sprinted to my car, backed up and left the scene.

I could dress normally — wear what I would wear in the States — in Sharjah, which would not have been the case if I lived in the neighboring country of Saudi Arabia to the west. Instead of being completely trapped in a full-length, black *chador* and veil, I was free to wear what fit my personality. The culture here did not force me into a uniform, and I felt a small sense of freedom every time I went into my closet to decide what I was going to wear. Being able to wear what I wanted allowed a small part of me, per-haps the American part of me, to roam wild without cultural fences. This didn't mean others felt comfortable with it, however. Since I was tall, with long blond hair and matching long legs that were not covered, I was stared at all the time, in a culture that did not encourage staring. This happened whenever I was out in public, whether I was walking or driving in the car. I took it all in stride and went about my business, though I made sure I never idled. Soon most everyone knew who I was, and I never felt frightened of being accosted.

Sharjah was beginning to feel like home, because I was determined to make it my home. I didn't keep wishing to go back to the States, instead tried each day to embrace this new culture by learning more of the language and customs. Some say *"home is where the heart is,"* but for me, *"home is where the head is."* This was going to be home. Period. I was going to make it work because this was where my husband lived. My heart wasn't in it when we were without electricity and water. My heart wasn't in it in the summer temperatures that hovered around 120 degrees with 100% humidity and made living unbearable for most foreigners. My heart wasn't always in it, but my head was. Instead of complaining about lack of water, I played a game with myself to see how fast I could shower. Because I knew the water could stop at any time and I'd end up with soap in my hair, I learned to shower in two minutes, long hair and all. When the electricity went out (which was often) during dinner and the windows were steamed because of the high humidity, we'd sit at the dinner table, as quietly as we could, and stare at each other until the air came on. Once there was no water or electricity for three straight days and the heat was well over 120 degrees. We were almost ready to move to the Sharjah Carlton when the air conditioning finally came back on.

My heart wasn't always in the Muslim culture either, but my head was. I endured the 30 day fast during the month of *Ramadan*. I did it for two reasons. First, I wanted to respect the Muslim religion, and second, I wanted to see if I could do it. It turned out to be easier than I thought because my head was in it.

Maher's parents observed the holy month of *Ramadan* very strictly, thus so did everyone in the household. We fasted from the start of dawn to the setting of the sun. I celebrated my first *Ramadan* in Beirut, in the midst of the war, even though the fighting threatened our safety and interrupted our daily schedules. I had fasted before in the Catholic Church for brief periods, so it wasn't totally new to me, and I wanted to show Maher's family that I could do it. During the daylight hours, Muslims totally abstain from food, drink, smoking and marital sex. You had the option of rising early in the morning to have a pre-fast meal (*suhoor*) before dawn. I didn't do that often, but if I knew I had a long day ahead of me I would occasionally have a little something (think *halawa*). I do remember more than once, however, when the fighting calmed down, going out to the balcony to wait for the setting of the sun (because I was hungry!).

It was common to eat dates (*iftar*) after sundown, followed by the sunset prayer, which in turn was followed by dinner. Since everyone was having dinner at the same time during *Ramadan*, it was not uncommon for Abu Nouman to invite other friends (when it was safe enough to travel) for this evening meal.

If you were sick or didn't feel well during *Ramadan*, you were exempt from fasting. You simply joined in later as you were able.

The month of *Ramadan* changes every year because it is based on the lunar year. Traditionally it starts when you can actually see the first crescent that follows the ninth new moon of the year. Muslims can also follow the calculated time of the moon, or the Saudi Arabian declaration, to determine the beginning and ending of the month.

The purpose of *Ramadan* is for Muslims to reflect on their lives and to experience a renewal of intense worship and of doing good deeds. Also, it is to remind them of the experience of hunger

My necklace spells *ma sha Allah* which means "God be with you"

and to be thankful for *Allah's* generosity. Maher's parent's observed all the obligated prayers. Maher did not do the actual prayers, nor did he observe the "call to prayer," though he did fast.

Ramadan is followed by *Eid-ul-Fitr*, the "festival of breaking fast." This celebration is marked, incidentally, the same way as the beginning of *Ramadan* — by the sighting of the new moon.

The only difficult situation I had with Arabic customs and food occurred during my second *Ramadan* in the Gulf. A baby lamb had just been killed and its beating kidney was brought to my plate. I had always eaten everything brought to me, always, as this is important in the Arab world. I looked at the kidney, still warm and still beating. I knew for sure my heart was not in this. I cut a small piece of the kidney and put it in my mouth as everyone at the table watched. I suddenly spit it out and ran from the table.

I was mortified. Even though I couldn't help what I had done, I felt like I had let Maher and the other people down. Had I made an unforgivable, social blunder? Maher told me later that I was forgiven. It was the first time I had not eaten what was put in front of me.

Shortly after this, I decided to start entertaining at our home, since having people over to eat was the highest form of hospitality. I began small — a dinner for nine that included Maher's boss, his family and friends. This would put me to the test, preparing a traditional Arab meal to people who know how to judge good Arabic cooking. I went to the *souk* and picked fresh vegetables and fruit by myself, thankful for the skills I had learned from Abu Nouman in

Beirut. I told the merchants I was preparing my first Arabic meal for guests, and not just my husband. They were so happy — I don't know if for them or me. I think they had been watching my progress as far as adapting to their country and were pleased that I had taken this next step.

I cooked all day because it was Arabic food, which needs to be done from scratch and simmer for many hours. I was so nervous I couldn't eat. I felt that a flop meant humiliation not just for me, but for my husband as well. I was determined I could indeed cook Arabic food and entertain other Arabs in my home. I needed to do this to be part of the land and its customs. For dessert I decided on a touch of Americana. I made banana cream pie and it was perfect. I was ecstatic the dinner turned out to be a success. Maher appeared to think it was no big deal — he knew I could do it. It wasn't just a meal to me, however. It was an initiation into the Muslim culture as an equal, at least among women. I felt a tinge of pride, too, because I was not just an American now. I was half Arab. My determination from head was now turning into heart.

Souk

Chapter Nine

Arabian Days

On March 1976, I received ten letters from my family that were sent to Beirut. I was so happy to hear from all of them: Sue and Randy (one of my sisters and her husband), my mom and dad, my best girlfriend, Suzi, and my grandparents. They were dated as far back as July of last year but it didn't matter. It was like unfolding precious silk to read their words, my heart connecting with theirs though separated by distance and time. For a few brief moments, we were all together.

I was getting used to the daily customs, with the main meal being in the middle of the day. Friday was the Muslim holy day so no one worked. On Fridays, Maher and I would go out for dinner and travel to a city nearby, usually Dubai or Abu Dhabi. They were the big cities of the Gulf and had many more stores than

Sharjah. The cities were beautiful and I especially enjoyed the palm trees, which the ruler of Abu Dhabi had imported. The *Corniche* (Street) on the water in Abu Dhabi was breathtaking. The shoreline seemed endless and the tall, stately palm trees seemed perfect next to the blue sea.

Rubab (Ruby), Maher's youngest sister who lived in Saudi Arabia with her husband, Sadallah, came to visit. Everything went well. For Rubab, visiting us was much easier living than in Saudi Arabia, where women had to cover themselves in public. She rather enjoyed the Emirates. My mother-in-law also planned to visit but a visa was not forthcoming for her maid, Umm Saad, so she refused to come. I thought it was ridiculous that she had to have her maid to visit family, but I knew I must respect the fact that she had her reasons, whether personal or cultural. Perhaps bringing her maid was a way of helping us.

When we didn't have visitors, I enjoyed going to the beach. One day a man who was the advisor to the Sheik of Sharjah tried to reach me by phone. He was trying to locate me because I was American. Guess where he found me? On the beach! It seemed that everyone knew Mrs. Tarabishi was in the sun on the beach at the Sharjah Carlton every morning. Apparently a good friend of his worked for a company who needed a qualified person. Would I please go in for an interview? I did — and that was that.

I worked for the Crescent Petroleum Company in Sharjah, a Texas-based oil company. Robert McMichael, Director of Financial Administration, was my boss. He was an American. The president of the company was an Arab, a very educated, good man. His office and reception area made up the entire second floor and had magnificent furniture. We did not see him often, but he was pleased to have me there because of my Arabic. The company ownership was 51% local and 49% American. It was the standard way businesses operated in the Gulf. No company could be a majority ownership unless it was locally owned.

The Crescent Petroleum Company was located in a beautiful, two-story building that was white and very modern. I worked with the oil riggers, who, after being on an offshore rig for 30 to 40 days, would report to my office. I would be the first person they met on shore before returning to the States. They were rugged, deeply tanned men who worked hard and long hours. They were wild, roughneck guys, but each had a heart of gold. It was funny that I had to come to Sharjah in the United Arab Emirates before I ever heard a southern accent. At first I couldn't understand them at all. Even though they had a great sense of humor, I had to maintain a straight face and try to keep them in order. It was not unusual to arrange flights back to the States through Amsterdam for a night.

Our department was the "hub" of the company. American expatriate employees were in and out of my office daily. They were recruited in the States to come and work in Sharjah. There were 19 American families and it was a big family atmosphere — everyone liked each other. No family ever lasted more than a year though — living here was difficult for the women and young children. They preferred to go back to the States. Mr. McMichael, however, lived many years in the Gulf with his family.

One of my favorite moments was flying in the open helicopter to see the rig and the men. I had never been in a helicopter, much

Imagine me in a helicopter

Baraka I

less one without doors. The air was very warm and the movement of the wind made it pleasant. I could see the huge open flame as we neared the rig, named the *Baraka I*. Dropping down on the rig was smooth and I was impressed with the pilot's skill. The working atmosphere was dangerous and exciting. The workers gave me a tour and seemed to appreciate my interest. They were all smiles, but they were busy and kept moving, nodding in approval.

My job at the Crescent Petroleum Company turned out to be one of the most rewarding work experiences I ever had.

An Arab woman invited me to the beach. I went to her home first, which was a huge villa, for coffee. I entered through the entrance for women, into a part of the home that was only for women and entertaining women. No men were allowed. She was an educated woman who was married to a local man and followed strictly the customs of this Muslim country. In the safety of this part of the home, she could remove her *chador* and dress normally. We had our coffee and *baklava* and then pro-ceeded to the beach, which was just outside, with a couple of other Arab women.

So on go the *chadors* and we walk to the sea. Since we were alone and no men were present, I figured they would remove their *chadors*. I removed my top and pants to expose a burgundy French bikini underneath. As I was doing this I watched the women walk straight into the water with their *chadors* on. They were quite comfortable with themselves and I was quite comfortable with myself, so in I went. They loved the water and were splashing and cooling off in the extreme heat and so was I. By the look on their faces, they couldn't believe what I was wearing and by the look on my face, I couldn't believe what they were wearing. We all laughed and enjoyed the beautiful smooth sandy beach.

It was August 1976, and by now I was getting used to driving everywhere. I had, however, one bad habit. Sometimes I would forget to make sure my gas tank was at least a quarter full. Maher warned me all the time never to have less than a quarter tank. I was getting a birthday cake for him from a new store that opened up and I ran out of gas. Big trouble. I was kicking myself for not being more careful, especially knowing that it didn't take long to get lost in the desert. I was in the middle of nowhere with no phone in sight, so I got out of my car and started walking.

I soon chanced upon a large tent. Perhaps I would not die in the desert after all. I announced my presence at the tent opening, saying *"Marhaba"* (Hello) over and over until someone finally came out. I was ushered into the tent without a word, as I crossed the threshold it was as if time suddenly reversed half a century. A large Bedouin family sat in a circle, filling most of the tent. My eyes flitted unconsciously, surveying the space and moving from person to person. The Bedouins I remembered had large, curved swords used for slicing and hacking — or was that just a scene from an old movie? I relaxed when I saw a single item positioned in the middle of their circle, an item that told me they were prosperous — an ancient, black desk telephone. It had a very long extension cord that ran outside of the tent.

Odd, I thought. I wonder where the cord goes. I didn't see any telephone poles nearby. Was it connected to another Bedouin's tent miles away? Perhaps it was hooked up to a camel-powered cell out back, or a satellite and cost $100 a minute. Perhaps it didn't work, but was merely placed as a status symbol for motorists like me stranded in the desert. And if it took two years to get a phone installed in Beirut, how long did it take to get one installed out here in the desert?

I was hoping and disbelieving at the same time. I was tempted to rush to the phone and call Maher before anyone could stop me, but I remembered the culture and waited without a word. After a full minute, I finally asked in Arabic if I could use the telephone please, explaining that I ran out of gas. Since they used camels, I didn't think they would be too sympathetic with my gas-guzzling problems. I was motioned to kneel down on one of the rugs, like everyone else. I watched the male head of the family closely, my head slightly bent down, carefully avoiding direct eye contact, waited for his signal of *aay wa* (yes) or *la' a* (no). I could see the others were very curious but never moved, they just sat or knelt and looked at me. Could it be I was the first blonde woman they had ever seen?

The head of the family made his decision, nodding his head ever so slightly toward the phone. I picked it up and called Maher. I spoke quickly and briefly, watching them watching me. I hung up and thanked them in Arabic. I stood up slowly and politely left, promising myself I would never run out of gas again.

They hadn't said a single word. And yet, in the harshest of environments in a foreign land, a strange family took pity on a strange woman. That, to me, spoke volumes.

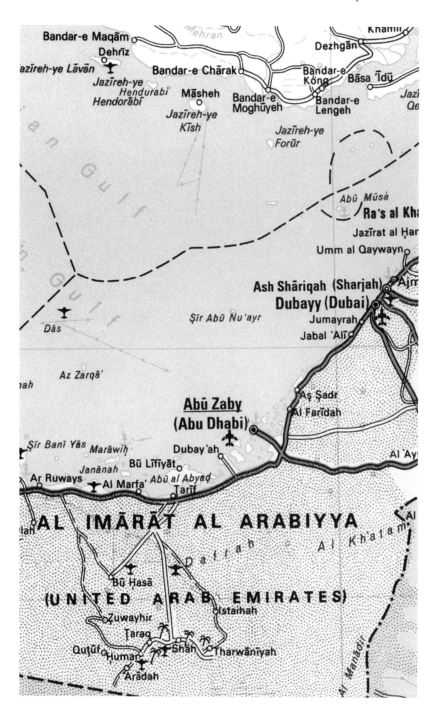

Chapter Ten

Riches of the Middle East

We spent the entire month of September 1976 in Italy. We were there because Maher needed to visit a number of Italian marble factories. We rented a Jaguar — British racing green. We visited the cities of Marina de Massa, Forte di Marmi, Massa, Viareggio, Marina de Carrara, Verona and Rome. Verona was one of my favorites. We attended a marble fair there and saw the Coliseum and the Tombs. Verona is the city of Romeo and Juliet with beautiful squares in the city where people gathered to listen to the musicians. I bought a sterling silver cigarette case, a case for matches and a small round plate. It was a set, each with a gold grape leaf on it. (Maher smoked but I did not.) I also bought six sterling silver cocktail stirrers, a sterling silver holder for a single rose and a tiny sterling silver bouquet basket. They were treasures to take back to Sharjah and our new apartment.

As nice as Verona was, I shall never forget Rome. To see the works and sculptures of Michelangelo, to see the marvel of St. Peter's Cathedral, to stand before the famous Wishing Fountain and throw my coins and make my wish, to shop at the Spanish Steps, to see the Square of the Three Fountains, to taste the luscious food and wine of Rome and experience it all on the arm of my lover was indeed paradise. I wrote to my family, trying to convey in words what I had experienced, but words were inadequate.

I returned "home" to Sharjah on October 5 while Maher stayed another three weeks and traveled to Sicily. Though we had moved to Sharjah just nine months earlier, I felt comfortable returning there to my new homeland.

I returned to my work because I was going to travel again to the States for Christmas and I had to count my vacation days. It would be my first visit back since arriving in Beirut over a year and a half ago. I was ecstatic to think about celebrating Christmas in my parent's home in Neenah and seeing all my family again.

At my parents' home with my siblings, but without Maher

My trip to the States in December and January '77 was different than what I thought it would be. I discovered that when I returned to Sharjah, I was returning home. I had visited my "childhood home" in the States, but it was no longer my real home. I tried to explain how life was in the Middle East. I told my family of the war in Beirut but that I was safe now in the Gulf. No one seemed to quite understand. I believe they took it all in and were grateful I was now in the Gulf.

The plane couldn't carry me fast enough back to Abu Dhabi and the arms of my husband. Strangely enough I found that I had missed the smooth, milky desert. Though harsh, it was breathtakingly beautiful and unlike anything I had ever known. It could be treacherous because of the *tuz* (sandstorms) and heat, but it was beautiful nonetheless.

The trip back to Wisconsin had been the right thing to do. I had missed Christmas and my family last year and Maher knew if I had not gone home to the States, I would have been deeply sad. The going over made the coming back profound in its meaning to my life. I knew now I wanted to spend the rest of my life here in the Middle East. Maher and I agreed that the next trip to the States would be together, or not at all.

By now two years had passed since arriving in Beirut. My whole life had changed. From the food I ate, to the language I heard and spoke, to the customs of the culture I lived in, to the weather I endured. Not one thing was the same for me; I had been transformed into this new woman, willingly and lovingly. I was melting into this land and culture. What I had learned and experienced seemed to strengthen my character, like adding layers of skin to my body. I was happy with who I had become and looked forward to each new day.

Maher was offered a job as manager of the factory for Marblo in Abu Dhabi, the capital of the United Arab Emirates and thought to be the most prosperous. It was a good move for him and his career. They asked him to give an answer immediately, but Maher said no — he would have to talk with me first. I could plainly see on his face how happy and excited he was. We discussed it and he called shortly after with his acceptance. I was

My last day

extremely proud of him.

I knew the last day of my job would be sad. I came to work and sat down in my chair wondering what I would actually do today. I looked around at the office, the largest and most beautiful I had ever had. I would miss it. But surprise! A champagne party had been arranged — the first ever in the office. I don't know if office drinking parties were legal, but I wasn't asking any questions! I was so happy they would even think to do this for me.

The Accounting Department, which was outside my office and across the aisle, was occupied by many well-educated employees from India. The chief accountant, Hamid, was a tall, soft-spoken man with a larger physique than most Indians. Actually, it was his belly that was large. When he spoke he always tilted his head, as is common with Indian nationals. He also walked with his head down and worried all the time, even when it seemed there was nothing to worry about. It was just his nature. My goal was to make Hamid smile. The Indian nationals were all very talented and worked hard. They sent most of their money back home to India for their families. During the party they presented me with a beautiful pair of opal and diamond earrings. I was surprised and honored and still have them.

I had hoped to open my own boutique in Sharjah. I had a local partner and everything was set to go just before Maher's promotion surfaced. But I wasn't upset. I figured there was something else in store in Abu Dhabi.

I was beginning to feel like myself around Abu Dhabi, which

was much larger and greener than Sharjah, but not as friendly — or so I thought in the beginning. It would just take some time. Our new apartment was very nice, even better than the one in Sharjah. Maher started to smoke cigars. They were a

20,000 dirhams for dinner

status symbol for men and the owner of Marblo only smoked very expensive cigars. I guess Maher was beginning to think of himself as a big shot, so even though he faked it, he too "smoked" cigars. I laughed at him and he laughed too.

We celebrated our second anniversary at the Hilton Hotel's Pearl Restaurant, a first class restaurant with international and Arabic food. The wine was imported from Paris and Italy. Dining in Abu Dhabi was reportedly the most expensive in the world. It was truly exceptional.

The owner of Marblo was entertaining businessmen and friends and invited Maher and me. We sat at an elegantly prepared table — about 10-12 of us. I was the only woman. Everyone wore business suits and I wore a beautiful dress. The service was out-standing. We had Perrier water, Russian caviar, Cuban cigars, trays of rare cheeses, fruit, flaming desserts and as much Dom Perignon champagne as we could drink. Maher told me later that the bill was 20,000 *dirhams* (about $20,000). My goodness, I thought. I should pinch myself to make sure I'm really not dreaming.

One of my favorite things to do was to go out for dinner and entertainment. Entertainment was allowed only in hotels. My favorite was belly dancing. I loved watching the dark beauties with light brown skin and long dark hair, moving their bellies so

I loved to watch the belly dancers

skillfully and gracefully as if all in one motion; bellies moved out unnaturally far, then brought in so tight you could see each distinct rib bone. Their costumes were made of gold threads that sparkled and enhanced their dark beauty. The Arabic music and dance was mesmerizing. I fell in love with the music, especially with Fayrouz, the legendary female Lebanese singer.

We soon became the couple to watch — Maher, the handsome Arab and his very fair American wife. We were noticed everywhere we went and I believe Maher loved this status. In all fairness, so did I.

I found an excellent hairdresser in one of the hotels who spoke English. She had a thriving business and was becoming very well-known to both the foreigners and Arabs who lived there. She was Lebanese, I believe. I needed her for trimming my long hair and for

Maher and me

putting it up on special occasions. She loved experimenting with my hair as it was so different from what she was used to. She told me it was easy to work with my hair because it was not the thick, curly hair that was sometimes unmanageable. She did her best work on my long, straight hair, she confided, and said in the same breath that she didn't know why, but that was just the way it was. We laughed. She was very lively, enthusiastic and charming. She wore bright colors — she was a bright color, and I so enjoyed her.

My hairdresser's work

One day, a *sheikha* (the wife of a sheik) came in with her entourage and sat down across the room. The hairdresser, of course, went to the *sheikha* to welcome her and ask what she would like done. The hairdresser returned to me shortly and placed herself in front of me so the *sheikha* could not see my face. She then whispered to me, "The *sheikha* would like to buy a foot of your hair, Madame." Thank goodness she was standing in front of me as I'm sure my reaction would have given me away. I leaned into her and whispered very discreetly, "What? Are you crazy?" Then she said, unfazed, "And she will pay you 20,000 *dirhams*!" "What?" Now I was way past astonished. Twenty thousand *dirhams* was about $20,000. I pulled myself together and said, "Please tell the *sheikha* that I am truly honored but I cannot do so at this time." I thought frantically and then added, "My husband would not be happy if I had it cut, but again tell her that I am very honored that she likes my hair." The hairdresser left and passed on my wishes to the *sheikha*. There was no further discussion or contact, nor were there hard feelings. If I knew anything about this culture, it was that the wishes of a husband should not be taken lightly — something I'm sure she had experienced for herself.

Chapter Eleven

Abu Dhabi Prison

One very hot day in August, I was driving slowly along a road in Abu Dhabi. It had been roped off on both sides with newly planted bushes inside the ropes. I saw no pedestrians at all and didn't expect to see any. Suddenly, out of nowhere, a young Arab woman stepped out into the road. I had no time to react, and I hit her with my car. She bounced off the windshield and I stopped immediately, horror-stricken. I jumped out of the car to help her. She seemed to be all right with little more than a bump and cut to her forehead; still, it was awful. She wore a headscarf and ordinary long clothes so I knew she was not a local Arab. (I later learned she was Palestinian.) As luck would have it, there was a local policeman close by. He helped me place her in the back seat of my car. We rushed to the local hospital, the police officer sitting directly behind me. He spoke no English.

In this country, if you are involved in an accident and injure a person who goes to the hospital and has to stay, then you must spend the same amount of time in jail. I had no idea what would happen once we got to the hospital. The young woman was being treated; I was told to sit and wait. I didn't like the waiting, nor did I like the thought of going to prison here. I had heard the stories — people going to jail and never being seen again. Spending time in jail, even for a night, was not just an idle threat — it could be a death sentence. I started to panic on the inside, knowing that I had to contact Maher.

All of a sudden there was a great commotion in the hospital. People were yelling. Commands were shouted. From what I could gather, there was a big accident on the desert road between Sharjah and Abu Dhabi. People were running, sirens were wailing. This was my chance to get to a phone. If I didn't, I knew all could be lost. They could take me away to a jail and even my own husband would never know. I snuck into a nearby room while the commotion was going on and there it was — an old black desk phone sitting in the middle of a very plain metal desk — the only two things in the room. I dialed Marblo, asked for Maher and quickly told him to get to the hospital before they took me somewhere.

I hung up and quickly went back to where I was supposed to be sitting. Two police officers came and stood in front of me. *"Yella"* (Let's go), they said. I could see the young woman had a large bandage on her forehead, but she was being released because her injuries were not serious. Then why were they taking me away? I knew protesting would do nothing other than harm my chances of getting help, so I remained quiet but very scared. I willed myself to be calm, even as the officer opened the back door of the police car for me to get in. I moved slowly, trying to stall for time and think about what I could do.

As the police car left the hospital, so did my hope. This is it. No one is ever going to find me. It's too late. I desperately tried to think when I heard the screeching of tires behind me. I turned around to look out the rear window and saw Maher's good friend, Marwain, driving the Marblo company car with Maher beside him. Marwain was a fellow Marblo manager who had lived here for many years and had lots of connections. As they rounded the corner to the hospital, I could see my husband's eyes. He was scared too. It was too late to stop the police car, so they followed. The air exhaled from my lungs; he knew where I was — he had gotten here just in time.

It was a long drive in the hot desert. Time stood still for me — I really could not determine how long we had been driving but it seemed forever — perhaps three-fourths of an hour. We stopped and a large prison with a high stone wall loomed before me. Maher and Marwain jumped out of their car and ran up beside me before the police car had stopped. They identified themselves and then protested my arrest. They tried to get me free, but their protests did nothing. Neither of them were local Arabs. Maher's boss was not in the country and the sheik he knew was also out of the country.

The police took me inside the prison. I stood in the court-yard knowing this was real, yet not believing it was happening to me. They escorted me to the women's side of the prison. I hoped and prayed Maher would think to call the American Embassy.

The guards kept staring at me. Was this the first time they had seen a white, foreign woman? I began to protest that I was an American citizen and insisted on a phone call to the American Embassy. I seemed to remember that from some movie. I thought it was worth a try, but they would hear nothing of the sort. No matter how many times I insisted, they ignored me.

Four short, thin guards in dark fatigues ordered me to walk forward. I did so reluctantly, not wanting to go farther into the prison. Like going into the belly of a whale, I knew the deeper I went, the harder it would be to get out. We stopped in front of a room and the guards motioned me in. I fought not to go, but by this time they had lost their patience and pushed me in.

I ended up with my back to the wall on the left side of the room. The guards left and my attention diverted to the deep brown eyes watching me. There were six of us in this 10' x 8' room — the size of a small bedroom. The other women were young — all of them, with long dark hair and nothing covering their heads. There was absolutely no expression in their faces, yet they kept staring at me, slowly moving closer. What were they thinking? I was suddenly aware that I had no bra on. Had they ever been this close to a white woman before? Were they just curious about me, or waiting for my next move?

I quickly scanned the room. The floor was part concrete and part dirt. To my right in the corner was a hole in the ground — the toilet, but no toilet paper. Two empty steel cots with filthy thin mattresses and no sheets or pillows were pushed against the wall. A chrome chair with a broken plastic seat was near me, so I grabbed it, pushing the back against the wall. I sat down, keeping my eyes on the other women, and slowly pulled my red and white striped summer dress over my knees. The ties at the shoulder seemed to disappear and I felt suddenly naked.

The air was still and hot — it was 120 degrees but there was no odor. No sound. No window except for a long, 4" wide rectangle at the top of the wall beyond anyone's reach — for air.

One of the women knelt at my feet. I felt like I had to act, to do something to break the silence and the stares. "Is there anything to eat?" I asked in Arabic. I could see there was a small, banged up, dirty refrigerator in the left-hand corner from the door. One of the women opened it to reveal a piece of stale Arabic bread curled up at the corners. Nothing else. The women remained unemotional — like nothing mattered and they didn't care. The tension increased. I had to try something else.

I took the left hand of the women kneeling near me and placed it on my breast. I looked her in the eye and said in Arabic, "See, I'm just like you — only white." A brilliant smile exploded on her face and the other women smiled; a few even laughed. I could feel the relief in my entire body, but I kept it to myself. The night would be bearable after all, no matter what happened.

It was getting late and I could see that daylight was almost gone. The guards came to the door and hurried all of us out of the room and into another next door. It was a larger room in length and we could lie down on the floor to sleep. We had a mat to sleep on and I sat there, waiting …

At 11:00 p.m. there was a commotion at the gate. Maher had called the American Embassy and was with the consulate. She was in a long white evening gown, obviously from attending a dinner or party of some kind. She didn't seem to be doing very well with the local Arabs either. She was allowed to see me and told me that unfortunately, I would have to spend the night. She would get me out in the morning. She also said that they would not allow my husband or anyone else to see me. I think she tried hard to be convincing, so I tried hard to believe that I would only be spending one night. The other female prisoners seemed surprised that someone was actually trying to get me out — as though they had accepted their fate that no one would help them. They simply put their heads down and went back to sleep. I remained awake the entire night. I was not anxious anymore about my safety, just anxious that this ordeal would end.

The next morning I was outraged. How could this be happening? We were allowed outside in the courtyard, so I began to be very loud and disruptive, insisting that I be let go or at least allowed to make a phone call. While I was wondering if they were used to this kind of behavior from a woman, a police officer came and took me out. Now what — was I being punished for my misconduct? Where were we going?

The police escorted me outside, then drove me back to the police station where Maher, Marwain, the American consulate and a host of other people were waiting. The consulate had been furious about the situation, especially when she learned that I was refused a phone call. She said she was going to have that changed.

I was exhausted and have never been so thirsty in my life. I had been given no food or water in prison. I later learned I would have had to spend at least another day and night in prison if it had not been for Maher and the others pushing for my release. It was frightening to think that without someone pulling for you on the outside, you could just disappear in this country. I could have spent months in that jail and no one on earth would have known — if I had not made that one phone call. I wondered about the other women left there. I asked Maher if there was anything we could do for them. He said no — their husbands probably put them there and they would most likely remain there until they wanted them out.

Chapter Twelve

Precious Memories

Everyone in Maher's family reunited in Beirut in October 1977, and it was very pleasant. Ruby came from Saudi Arabia (her husband had to depart the same day we arrived), as did Nouman (Maher's older brother), and Nadia came from Paris. Maher and I came from Abu Dhabi on a business vacation. Maher's mother was so happy to have us all together.

It had been nearly a year since we had left Beirut. The people and the land had gone through so much hell, yet both refused to die. In fact, the city seemed to be thriving in some areas. You could still sense the fearful caution, however, from those who knew how quickly violence could erupt. There had never been a more beautiful city to me than Beirut. But now, like sterling silver, it had become tarnished by the careless touch of man.

Some areas of Beirut miraculously escaped physical destruction — like Hamra Street where all the cafés were. It was bustling with life again, but only during the day. Before, this busy and popular street would be full until 3 or 4 a.m. Now at night, the streets of Beirut were deserted. (The nightclubs were still full. The young people loved to party in Beirut.) The peacekeeping forces were everywhere, on every corner, on every street and at many of the roadblocks. It was important to carry your passport at all times for identification. Every once in awhile you could hear a distant explosion, which in turn erupted old memories and fears.

I brought a trunk from the States that contained a few personal items when I first moved to Beirut. We had left it behind when we fled and now I was able to take it home with me to Abu Dhabi. A few precious things, like a decorative tablecloth, a candle, a book and some pictures. Just little things from home, yet things that brought happy memories to mind. After being back in Beirut, I understood how important it was to hang on to those happy memories. Sometimes, the memories are the only things that give us meaning to enrich our lives.

A month after returning from Beirut I was not feeling well. Not really sick — my body just felt off. My stomach felt nauseated and the growth and hardness of my breasts was getting ridiculous. I became suspicious that I might be pregnant. I didn't have a doctor here, but I remembered a friend of mine had given me the phone number of a gynecologist in Abu Dhabi. Surprisingly I kept the number. Two days later, I brought in my urine sample.

That day Maher was in the Sharjah factory. Someone from the company had driven me to the doctor's office because my car was being repaired. The entire day I kept walking up to the mirror and looking at myself and saying, "I'm going to have a baby." I cried again and again throughout the day, overwhelmed at the miracle that I carried inside me.

The phone rang. It was Maher, telling me he would be home about 8 p.m. I tried to make dinner reservations at the Hilton Hotel but they were booked full because of a government delegation. So I planned the next best thing — maybe the best thing really. I lit every candle in the house, believe me I had a few, then dressed in a beautiful long white gown. I poured two glasses of wine and placed them next to our bed, turned the lights out and unlocked the door.

Maher came into the room and sat by my side. When he asked how I was feeling, I pointed to the candle above my head. I had purchased the candle in Milwaukee before leaving home; I was going to light it in our first home after we were married. It was a white, thin sleek cat about 10 inches tall with rhinestones around its neck. It was one of the things I brought back in the trunk. After two years of war and storage it had remained untouched. Maher knew it would only be lit on a very special occasion. "You shouldn't light it — it's too beautiful," he said. I looked up at the candle. "Maher, last night I was thinking to myself that one day I would light that candle and it would be when I told my husband that I was going to have a baby." Then I looked back to Maher and said, "I'm going to have a baby." Tears were flowing freely down my cheeks. Maher's eyes sparkled in the night and he picked me up and held me. He was very, very happy. An hour later we called my family in the States.

Three months later, I finally received some pamphlets and a book from my mother on pregnancy, since I was at a complete loss and the doctor's office offered absolutely nothing for reading materials. My baby was due June 6. If I wanted to deliver my baby back in the States (and have the best hospital care), I had to be there at least four weeks before that time. So I planned my trip for May 5.

I was working again in Abu Dhabi, this time for Arthur D. Little. Our only client was the Abu Dhabi Petroleum Company. The company rented a villa and I was in charge of furnishing it. I also worked preparing contracts for my boss, contracts that were written in English and Arabic. I really enjoyed the job, but I would start showing soon and he would need time to replace me — a very hard thing to do.

On Easter Day, I was cooking with my gas stove (everything was gas here). I lit the oven, when I returned to check on it, it was out. I took another match and lit it again. There was a big explosion and the oven filled with a huge flame. I felt like I was boiling. My clothes had not caught fire but I was shaking, terrified for my baby. My hand and arm were burned and my hair and eyebrows were singed and crinkled. The smell was awful. I turned off the gas and put my hand and arm under running cold water — although even the cold water was warm because of the hot temperatures outside.

I ran for the phone and called Maher, who came home immediately. I was lucky. I was so anxious because of my baby that I had stomach pains. Maher made me lay down, putting ice on my hand and arm. Hours later the pain in my stomach was gone. How could I have been so careless? I resolved to be more careful in the future.

Chapter Thirteen

Raising a Daughter in the Middle East

I had lived in the Middle East for over three years. I was now leaving the United Arab Emirates for the States on May 5, 1978, to deliver my first baby. It was so exciting. I knew I would be fine traveling alone. I was strong, young and healthy. Everything was going well until I started to experience severe back pain between London and Chicago. The young, new stewardess tried to maintain a cool manner and said, "Don't worry Ma'am, we're trained to deal with this kind of thing." I thought to myself, "Yeah, right." The pain grew worse and I could see the panic in her face. This time it was me who put her at ease. I said, "Don't worry dear, I'm not in labor. I'll make it." She probably said to herself, "Yeah, right."

Our perfect daughter (aren't they all?) was born on June 17 at Theda Clark Hospital in Neenah, Wisconsin. She had beautiful olive skin—no red, wrinkly skin on this child. She was "toned." No spots to go away and she had lovely dark hair. Born in the States, she would have an American passport. I did not yet know how important that would be.

Maher and I had purchased a home in Appleton just before her birth. It was a new condo complex. We thought it would be a good investment if and when we decided to move from the Gulf. If the war was still going on in Beirut and we couldn't return there, we would have this place. Another fateful decision.

We named our daughter Nadine, a popular French name in Lebanon meaning "hope." French names were common since Lebanon had been a French colony. She was two weeks old when we traveled back to Abu Dhabi via Paris. She traveled well, breastfeeding was a joy and we were both very relaxed.

On the second leg of our trip from Paris to Abu Dhabi, Nadine was lying in front of me in a basinet attached to the bulkhead (wall). I leaned over to check on her and noticed she wasn't breathing. I picked her up and started pounding her back. Still she would not breathe. She was gasping for air but couldn't get any, as though she were choking. I continued to hit her back but nothing happened. A man nearby saw what was happening. I looked at him in desperation. He said, "Give her to me, I have two children of my own." I lifted her to him and he also started pounding her back — still nothing. He quickly gave her back to me and ran for a stewardess. They came running — all the stewardesses. One had been a nurse. She took Nadine, who just then started to breathe. I was never so happy to hear her cry. My little girl … I held her. I never laid her down again and I never slept. I just watched her sleep until we reached Abu Dhabi some 10 hours later.

We arrived the next day in Abu Dhabi at 8:30 a.m. It is a

custom in the Middle East that when a baby is born, friends and neighbors welcome the new baby into the world by bringing gifts. I couldn't believe they came so soon after arrival — the same day! The flat was a mess. Hundreds of cockroaches seemed to have taken over the place. I was a mad woman bent on making sure the house was clean and orderly for my new daughter. I was exhausted by the time Maher's boss, wife and Marblo employees arrived that evening, bearing gifts and thrilled to see Nadine. By the time I collapsed in bed that night, having been up most of the last 24 hours traveling, nursing and cleaning, I wondered if Arab expectations for hospitality didn't go a little overboard.

Nadine was a big eater. She wanted to nurse every two hours. It took her a full 45 minutes to eat so I was feeding her every 75 minutes. Keeping house while nursing 12 times a day has a way of changing things, but how rewarding. I lost a lot of weight and had to work at keeping it on.

Maher enjoyed being a new father. He played with our daughter and held her — until she spit up, that is. Then she became my daughter.

I wrote my mother to tell her she would be very proud of me and to let her know I thought I was going to be all right here on my own. I felt confident with my baby. All I needed was a little guidance from above.

I had a nice surprise at the end of the month when I received several back copies of National Geographic — April, May, June and July. My parents had given us a subscription two Christmases ago! They were lost in Beirut and Damascus and had finally made it to Abu Dhabi. What a treasure.

We traveled with Nadine to Beirut, Lebanon, in March 1979 to the new Tarabishi home. Maher's parents had decided it best to move to a different area — a safer one. All the brothers and sisters came to celebrate Mother's Day (March 21 in Beirut) and to get together. It was only Nadine that got the rough end of the deal. She was not used to all the strange new faces. It wasn't until the last day that she settled down and let her grandfather finally hold her.

The Tarabishi home was glorious in its spaciousness and grandeur. The marble floors were spectacular. We felt quite safe in this new neighborhood and Maher's father had a solid steel door installed over the regular door. I was happy to see that.

We returned to Abu Dhabi and discovered we had a Dairy Queen. It had always been one of my favorite restaurants in the States. Everything was imported, right down to the napkins. It reminded me of how much I had taken for granted living in the States. I decided I wasn't going to make the same mistake here. We went every Friday — I insisted. The DQ was a hit for others in Abu Dhabi as well — it was crowded from the day it opened.

The very first supermarket opened right across from our house in May. I was so excited I could hardly stand it. There were things I hadn't been able to get since arriving here two years ago. I went every day, just to make sure I didn't miss anything. Nadine loved it too.

We celebrated Nadine's first birthday with a very small party. Her first and only friend was Stephanie, who was the same age. Jane, her mother, was a sweet tiny American woman. We let the girls do whatever they wanted with the cake. Did they take advantage! Jane was my first close friend in the Middle East. On July 9, she went back to the States with her husband, who had worked for the American Embassy. I was very sad, but grateful for the nine months we had together. She was the only babysitter I would leave Nadine with as it was a perfect fit — a mom with a daughter the same age as Nadine.

Hot August was upon us, but an exciting shipment from the States arrived: a potty-chair. I put it in the bathroom for Nadine to get used to. She was delighted though she had no idea what it was for. She just played with it.

Birthday cake

Nadine still had a voracious appetite and ate everything we did. One evening we were having cashews and true to form, she had a few small pieces. Immediately I noticed red spots on her chin but thought nothing of it. At dinner she refused to eat or drink and became very irritated and hard to handle. When she fell asleep at 6:15 p.m. I was worried, but had no idea what was wrong. At 5:00 a.m. she started crying and I went in to peek; she was laying down and quiet. By 6:30 a.m. she was screaming in agony. I rushed to her, knowing I had to remain calm. Nadine had vomited and pieces of cashews were present. But worst of all, from head to toe, she was covered with a large, raised rash and her eyes were swollen. She was completely bloated — her entire body. I called Maher, for inside I was hysterical.

Nadine refused food or drink again. There were no doctors available until 8:30 a.m., so the only thing I could do was to strip her and bathe her in cool water. She screamed the whole time. The doctor said it was an allergy rash, and of course we knew it was the cashews. I was relieved. Nadine didn't eat for hours but did drink lots of apple juice. By the next morning, she was fine.

On August 24, we left for Beirut. The city was in much better shape than it had been in March during our last visit. We actually could go out in the evenings. For the first time since Nadine's birth, we got to go dancing every night until 3:00 a.m. It was wonderful for the two of us to go out again. Shopping was back in swing in Beirut and the latest fashions from Paris were available and did we shop! It was fun to shop for Nadine's wardrobe also. We returned September 10 to Abu Dhabi.

Driving in the Gulf was totally different from driving in Beirut. Traffic in Beirut was always congested, with small cars everywhere and absolutely no rules. People parked wherever they could. If it meant driving up a curb between two cars and going in sideways, it didn't matter. People in Beirut also drove the wrong way on one-way streets — on purpose. No one seemed to care. In Abu Dhabi, however, there wasn't much traffic, so getting from one place to another didn't usually pose many hazards. Rather than intersections they had roundabouts. Each round-about had a monument or something special in the middle. There were no speed limits posted.

One day I was driving in my car, a white Buick, with Nadine in the front passenger side in her car seat. As I was veering right and going around a roundabout, a huge 18-wheeler truck came speeding alongside me. Suddenly my car was sucked underneath its belly. I kept one hand on the wheel and grabbed Nadine's car seat in the other and told her calmly that everything was okay. She was doing fine — it was me who was starting to panic. Our vehicles collided. Tires screeched. Metal scraped and screamed like tin scraps in a food processor before an ear-shattering boom belched us out. As quickly as we had gone underneath the truck, we were out, though it had dragged us a bit before breaking loose. The truck never stopped. I got off to the side of the road and just sat there in dis-belief. I took Nadine out of her seat to hug her. I pulled myself together and buckled her back in. No one had seen the accident.

Nadine

Not counting Beirut, Maher and I had only two chances to be out together without Nadine. Finding a babysitter in the Middle East wasn't like in the States where you could often find a responsible, caring teenager living close by. In fact, babysitters were rare because most people didn't use them. Instead they used their Indian or Pakistani live-in servants, which were so numerous and were also extremely cheap to hire.

Thus far, I had refused to have one even though I had a very large home. I still preferred to clean my own house, which everyone else looked upon unfavorably. I could only wonder what they thought. I did, however, have an Indian boy from Maher's office come once a week to wash the windows and balcony — that alone took him five hours. We were on the top floor of the building and had a balcony that went two full lengths of the penthouse with a spectacular view of the Arabian (Persian) Gulf waterfront. The Wisconsin house I grew up in could have easily fit into the living room, replete with white carpeting and lots of plants to give it a light and airy atmosphere.

After much searching, we finally found Iris. She was Chinese, single and 38 years old. She lived with relatives, who had lived in Oregon and were naturalized American citizens. She loved children and she passed my scrutiny. I was so cautious leaving Nadine that I would only be gone for two hours.

The other reason I refused to hire someone was that most of the Indians and Pakistanis were male. The most horrible crime took place in Abu Dhabi to an American couple with their 18-

month-old daughter the year before. The Indian boy who had lived with them for three years as a servant also babysat for them. He raped the baby girl and fled the country. The parents came home to a torn baby. There just were no words …

Being American posed other dangers for me and my child during this time. In November 1979, the American Embassy in Tehran, Iran, was overrun by a large group of students. I was very upset that this had happened and that the Americans were held hostage. Iran's border was only 175 miles from Abu Dhabi across the Arabian (Persian) Gulf. Maher warned me that I should not go out of the home. There were many Iranians living here. I lived here too, I insisted, and I wasn't going to stay home. I remember going to the *souk* (market) and though I felt secure, I became very aware of what was going on around me and who was close by. It was as though all my senses were heightened and constantly on alert, something that had started while we lived in Beirut during the civil war. The Middle East was a complicated place, and it paid to be aware of your surroundings at all times. This skill had served me well in the past and would continue to do so in the future.

We remained safe throughout the ordeal. The American hostages were held 444 days.

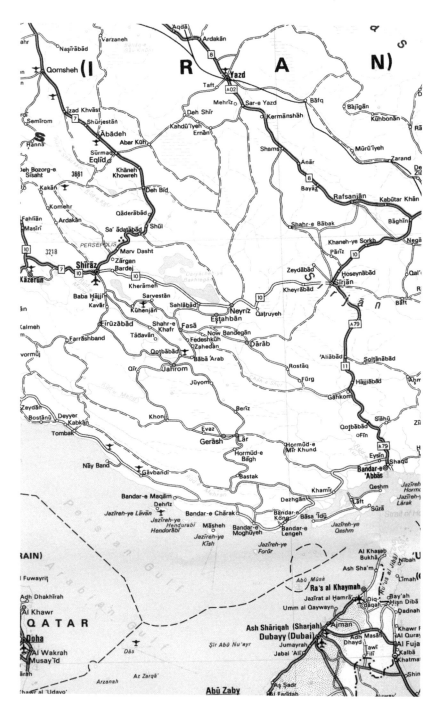

Chapter Fourteen

Giver of Life

In February 1980, I discovered I was pregnant again. As I struggled with my morning sickness, Nadine struggled with her potty training. She absolutely loved her potty-chair and carried it everywhere with her, especially when watching TV. We had an Arabic Sesame Street, which she adored. She placed the potty-chair in front of the TV, then stood in front of the potty-chair, backed up carefully, put her hands on the arms and carefully lowered herself. She then leaned back in her chair, making herself comfy as she watched TV — just like a big grownup.

Wherever I went, she followed with her potty-chair and set herself down until I finished whatever I was doing. Usually she'd take a book along with her so she could "read" while waiting for Mommy. I decided we had to get down to the "bare"

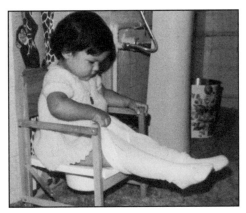

Nadine

facts of serious potty training. Now Nadine was sitting without pampers and loved this too. However, every time I would go to the bathroom, she wanted to go. This got a bit much, but I obliged.

Soon I couldn't get her off the potty. She wanted to be big, I guess. It was so cute. Then success! I was so excited you would have thought I just won the lottery when all my daughter did was pee in the right place! I guess you have to be a parent to relate. I praised her and praised her and clapped and clapped. It's fun and exciting this new stage in her little life, but how I dreaded the day when I'd have to admit she's no longer my little baby girl — that brought tears to my eyes.

On February 24, Maher left for business in Beirut. We understood that the situation was not good. In fact, areas of Beirut were deteriorating by the hour. I prayed for his safe return. In the meantime, potty training remained our main focus.

By this time, my Arabic, with a Lebanese/Syrian accent, was pretty good, though I had to deal with the various Arab dialects. The varieties of a speaker's mother tongue and everyday talk would vary from country to country in the Arab world. Knowing the language was a huge benefit to me in many ways. I must admit it was fun listening to the Arab men talking about me when they obviously felt confident I did not understand the language. One day, when I was on the elevator in our building with Nadine in the stroller, two young Arab men entered and stood behind us.

As we were leaving, one of the gentlemen said I was very beautiful. I strolled off the elevator, my back to them, then turned to meet their eyes. *"Shu kran ik teer,"* I said in Arabic (Thank you very much) and walked away. I wish you could have seen the expressions on their faces. Priceless.

While Nadine liked Sesame Street, I indulged once in awhile by watching Egyptian soap operas. The Egyptian women were very expressive, making American soap operas look like old black and white re-runs. They were over-dramatic and passionate, using shrill voices, flying arms and long, drawn-out, unending crying scenes to make their point. They wore bright scarves on their heads, brightly colored clothing and large jewelry. Still, I would be caught up in the drama, shaking my head and laughing. I had to admit, it was entertaining.

In April, I was in my fourth month of pregnancy and was beginning to feel better — with only mild morning sickness. I was very happy to be having another baby so that my children would be close in age, just two-plus years apart. And once again, I got to light my very special candle for my husband. This time there was no guessing on his part as to why the candle was lit. Once again, it was a precious moment.

It was time to find a doctor. There were only two doctors that treated pregnant women in Abu Dhabi. One was a GP, Dr. McCalluck. He became my doctor. The other was an obstetrician, but I'd heard some awful stories about her.

The small pool of doctors may have been the result of cultural differences more than anything else. Dr. McCalluck, a few years back, was examining a pregnant Arab woman (she was local, I believe). During the exam she cringed up, panicked and ran out of his office screaming, causing a scandal. Dr. McCalluck nearly lost his practice and swore he wouldn't touch another pregnant woman again. I can only guess that this woman was not used to being examined by a male doctor as we are in Europe and America.

Knowing many of the cultural differences, I did not let this incident interfere with my judgment about him. He was Egyptian and had an English mother, so his English was perfect. For that I was very grateful. I liked him instantly. He was of normal height and stature with salt-and-pepper hair and a short-trimmed beard and mustache. He was gentle and very considerate. He was friendly, yet very professional — all good signs. The checkup went well and everything appeared to be normal. Once again, I started sending letters to the States signed "Nancy+."

I woke one morning to spotting. I was alarmed. This never happened with Nadine. I immediately called Dr. McCalluck. He told me I must stay in bed. Since I had a toddler it just wasn't possible, so I cut down what I was doing. I continued to spot the next day and had no choice but to find someone to help me in the home while I stayed in bed.

The new maid was from Eritrea. She lived with other Eritrean friends so she came to the house in the morning and left after dinner. She had beautiful, glowing white teeth. She kept them clean by frequently chewing on a small twig. This was the way her people cleaned their teeth, she said. Remarkable, I thought. Perhaps dentists are overrated...

Once in awhile she wanted to cook herself food from Eritrea. The spices were so strong that even the smell from the kitchen was overpowering. She loved it, of course, so when she cooked Nadine and I made sure to keep clear of the kitchen.

Arabic food, in comparison, is not spicy in the sense of being hot like Indian curry or other hot spices. Typically, Middle Eastern spice means a combination of allspice with black pepper, cinnamon, nutmeg, cardamom, cloves, ginger and dried rose petals.

I continued to spot at the very least activity. Nadine was thoroughly disgusted with this new bedridden mom and pouted a lot. I disliked being in bed more than she did and had a difficult time staying there. But the thought of losing this child halfway through the pregnancy was unbearable, so I did what I was told.

I decided to call Dr. Darr, my doctor back in the States who had delivered Nadine, to make sure I was doing everything I needed to do to keep this baby safe. He confirmed Dr. McCalluck's orders — there was nothing I could do except stay in bed. He also told me, however, that I had to decide whether I was going to travel to the States now or stay and deliver in Abu Dhabi. If I waited too long, it would be too late and I would have to stay. I needed to make the decision that week. There were no hospitals here I felt comfortable going to. I weighed the fact that I could lose the baby on the plane, as Dr. Darr said.

Perhaps this was the first time I really listened to my body and what was going on inside me. I needed to trust my instincts. I needed to trust myself. I decided, very confidently, to go back to the States. I would take the chance now so that my baby had the best chance when it was delivered.

At five months pregnant, travelling by plane, I was restricted to a wheelchair the entire way. I stayed with my parents in Neenah until the birth of my son, Manar, born October 21. He was over 9 pounds and was two days late. They never thought I would make it past my seventh month. Maher was unable to be present for the delivery of our son. He had come over with Nadine and me because I needed to be in a wheelchair, but he couldn't stay the four months because of his job. Also, we did

Leaving the hospital with Manar

not want to travel back to the Middle East with a newborn and have the same problems we did with Nadine and her breathing episode. So timing was important; we decided he should meet us in the States shortly before we needed to return to our home in Abu Dhabi.

Manar was so different than Nadine. His skin was much fairer and he was a big baby. As I viewed him in the big window I heard other people say, "Look at the huge baby, he's half grown!" I just smiled. If they only knew the journey this little one had already been on, a journey he wasn't expected to make. His name Manar (an Arabic name) means "one who gives light." I knew he would be just that in his lifetime — a giver of light.

My days were filled with Nadine and Manar and I wrote less back to the States. Maher left every Saturday morning early and returned Sunday night late. He left again Tuesday morning early and returned late Thursday night. He was home on Fridays, the Muslim holy day, and on Mondays. He was working both factories — Abu Dhabi and Sharjah.

Everything I did with the children took a lot of planning and care. The sun was my biggest concern. There were no garages and finding shade was a miracle because there were very few trees, so cars heated up like ovens. With temperatures hovering around 120 degrees Fahrenheit, you could burn yourself on anything vinyl or metal just getting into the car if you didn't cool it off before getting in. With two squirming children it became a real challenge to drive anywhere. The cooler months were a joy with the children as we could go for walks. During the hot months of June, July, August and September, however, even taking walks was out of the question.

Manar was growing so fast I could hardly believe it. At this rate, he would soon be bigger than his older sister. At my doctor's appointment for Manar's three-month check up, the doctor told me I had to stop feeding Manar and give him only my milk, since he weighed

Manar

nearly 20 pounds. He was adamant and very worried. I laughed and told him that Manar was only getting my breast milk. He was astonished and said, "You better bottle and patent that milk of yours!" He paused, then said, "You could feed the village babies." I thought he was joking at first, but he said he knew of young mothers who had little milk. I told him I'd be glad to help, but I never heard anything after that.

In April 1981, we moved back to Sharjah so Maher could work full-time at the company's factory there. A villa was rented for us. This was, to me, the closest we had to a freestanding home like in the States. Even with all the money in the United Arab Emirates, most homes, like in Beirut, were apartments rented in a three or four-story building. Villas were now becoming popular, but they were expensive, so it was quite a surprise to receive this bonus from the company. Our villa had high stucco walls around the entire home. The wall was necessary for two reasons. First, it kept out the roaming animals of the Bedouins. And second, it kept the desert out. The *tuz* (sandstorms) were horrible and sand

Our home and garden in Sharjah

got into every window and door. It was much worse without a wall.

The front wall gate of our two-story home was enormous. It opened up to a long, wide walkway that led up to three wide steps of beige marble onto a marble porch before coming to the large wood front door of the house. The front porch was large enough for a covered, portable porch swing and made for a great play area. The ground was mostly sand at this time, but I envisioned a garden in the future. Bright purple bougainvillea was growing on the front gate and front wall. It seemed that the one flower that flourished in this heat was the bougainvillea. There were two large rectangular built-in planters at the inside of the front gate and at the steps on the porch.

I soon found a third purpose for the high stucco walls around our house. It allowed me to do my gardening in complete privacy — in my swimsuit. Not a big deal in the States, but a definite asset here in the Middle East. With temperatures in the 100s and going past 120 degrees in the summer, it was simply too hot to garden in any other kind of clothing. I watered every day from sunup to sundown; it was a full-time job.

Manar became a big, happy baby. He was in to everything

in our new home. Nadine was always tattling on him. There wasn't much he couldn't do. Even with the bedrail up, I didn't know how long it would hold him. He was just too strong.

Then at 11 months, over he went. So I put him to sleep in the playpen. We finally found a wonderful Italian bed (in one of the new furniture stores that was flourishing here in the Gulf) close to the ground with a foot-high railing for small children. He could easily get out and be safe at the same time.

Manar's new bed

Chapter Fifteen

Nos ou Nos
(Half American, Half Arab)

June got very hot — already in the 100s. We left Abu Dhabi for Europe to spend the summer and get some relief from the scorching summer sun for the children. Nadine was almost three and Manar was eight months old. Maher's parents joined us in Rome and Maher's brother, Nouman, had a flat with his family, which we visited.

Rome was everything I remembered. The food was delicious and the wine was so much a part of life that it became part of ours. Shopping in Rome was everything I had imagined, just like in the movies. It was extravagant, with all the latest fashions. I tried on dresses while Maher sat outside the large dressing rooms in a comfortable chair with a bottle of wine next to him. He could look at me and I could see a full view of each dress in the mirrors. The woman helping me tried to sell as much as possible by expounding on how lovely I looked. She must have been convincing because Maher bought many dresses. When I thought we were finished, Maher told me we now had to shop for shoes to go with each outfit! Italian shoes are exquisite. Some had very high heels with jewels in them, others were in bright colors, still others from famous designers had low heels. It seemed every shoe imaginable was there for my choosing. Life was indeed good.

Rome was also a very family-friendly city, for the most part.

Rome

Since we were staying for at least a month, we rented a flat, which gave us more room with the children. The weather in Rome was comfortable and pleasant, perfect for long strolls. I could push Manar's stroller with one hand and hold onto Nadine's hand with the other. One day as we were walking, someone pinched me on the derrieré. I looked quickly to find a young, handsome man smiling at me. I couldn't help but shyly smile in return and continue on. (Oh dear, this was common I was told.)

When I decided to have my hair done, I walked into a salon and a young Italian man invited me to sit down. He got down on his knees and said in broken English, "You are the first woman I have ever gotten down on my knees for." The men were quite charming — I decided not to tell my husband about that one, even though I was quite sure this was not the first time he had gotten down on his knees to cut hair.

One of our favorite things to do in Rome was to go to the café Doney (pronounced Don yeah). Nadine, Manar and I would go to this indoor/outdoor café late every morning. There were days when Abu Nouman, Umm Nouman and Maher would join us. I would have a cappuccino and Nadine would order a 7-Up. The waiter was a very handsome young man who came to adore Nadine and she him. It was always a fine time. I savored the innocence and luxury of it all.

Umm Nouman and Maher

After Rome, we went to Paris for a short time. We stayed in a flat on the Champs-Elysées, reportedly one of the most famous and beautiful avenues in the world. The flat was very old, but clean and lovely.

Nadine and me

Shopping here was very different from Rome. The women in the shops were very unfriendly and uninterested in helping me, which made things uncomfortable. I walked into one shop and no one helped me, so I walked out and looked into the window again at something I liked. Maher was just walking up, and when he saw what I was looking at, suggested we go back into the shop. Suddenly the women were interested in helping me and spoke English to boot! I said no to Maher and walked out. I think the women were very surprised and realized they made a big mistake.

I discovered other unpleasantries in Paris. As I was walking down the Champs Elysées very near our flat, a man stole my yellow diamond ring — lifted it right off my finger and I never felt a thing! I had just glanced at it seconds before and now it was gone. I was devastated, since this was Maher's mother's ring that he had given me on our wedding day. I learned to always keep my fingers bent and closed when in a large metropolitan city.

Seine River boat tour

The scenery in Paris was beautiful, however. We took the boat tour on the Seine River — a big adventure for the children — and it was magnificent. We could see many architectural marvels, like the twelfth century Notre Dame Cathedral. We also went to the Louvre Museum and saw the Mona Lisa. The Arc de Triomphe was a must see as well.

In August, we arrived back in Abu Dhabi to bad news. I had intended to write a glowing report of our summer only to find that my best girlfriend in Abu Dhabi, Adla, who was from Lebanon, had lost her sister. Her sister had been killed in Lebanon in the midst of the fighting. I went to see her immediately. She asked, "Why wasn't anyone doing anything?" I had no answer for her. I believe she was referring to the Americans doing something. How could the fighting still continue there? Though the war was far from us, it never escaped us.

I had no time to write to the States. Very often caring for the children just didn't seem to allow it. Manar was still not sleeping nights. During the day he was either breaking something or fighting with Nadine. Nadine could not accept the fact that some toys were Manar's; she thought they were all hers. Manar got very upset and bit Nadine. Everyone was crying … and on and on it goes.

Manar's first birthday

We celebrated Manar's first birthday. I was exhausted by night, but was determined to write back to the States with news of what was happening. I wrote:

> I don't think books are the complete answer. I'm sure they're very beneficial and I wish I had and could read some. Since my marriage and having children have all happened while living in the Gulf, I have not read a single book or pamphlet on child rearing and related subjects, simply because it is not available here. My motherly instincts are my only guideline. I have absolutely no one here to advise or help me. I must use my good judgment, common sense and love for my children. I feel, especially now that Nadine is old enough to understand, that talking is so important. We talk all the time — she is delightful to talk to.
>
> A day doesn't pass between me and Nadine that we don't tell each other how much we love one another. We hold each other always, or at least whenever I can pry myself from Manar, as he is extremely attached to me. Don't worry, Mom, I'm always watching Nadine and Manar out of the corner of my eye for any jealousy or sadness and try always to give both my attention. I even carry

both of them sometimes and they love it.

Nadine is my very precious little girl. She's my first-born. Our relationship is so special. I always told myself that if I ever had a daughter, I would love her so and she would know it. We would be so close. Well, now I have this gorgeous little daughter and it is so.

Now, about Manar's birthday. Maher was home and it was just the four of us. We had a little cake and presents for both children. Unfortunately, it was a rather bad day, right up until the moment of cake cutting and opening of presents. Nadine was at her worst. She could not accept Manar's birthday. She woke up sad knowing it was his birthday. I thought we had prepared her for this. She proceeded to school very upset and unhappy. Throughout the day, she pooped in her panties. And when Manar started to play with his new toys, she took them away. She was absolutely and totally unbearable. I couldn't believe it. She wasn't mean or nasty; it was as though she couldn't help herself. After all, she's the only one who ever celebrated a birthday, how come all of a sudden Manar's having one? I kept telling myself this is a normal reaction. But at the end of the day she came to me and said, "Mommy, I'm sorry. I'll be good tomorrow, but not today." I suppressed a smile and told her I was glad she was going to be good tomorrow (because I'd go crazy if she didn't!).

Now about Manar. He's absolutely the naughtiest boy in the whole world I'm sure! Never sleeps, is a complete mommy's boy, wants to be held always or else set free to do what he wants. He will not be confined to a playpen, bed or stroller. He is into everything. He walks into the kitchen and proceeds to take every single pot and pan out and pound them all on the floor. He loves noise — the louder the better. If a toy doesn't make noise, forget it! A stuffed, soft toy is not his idea of fun. He has broken crystal, cabinet doors, mattresses and bumper pads. Just yesterday (on his birthday) he broke a large decorative divider I had at the entrance that separates the dining area from the front door entrance. It was beautiful chrome with a delicate, lovely design on it. He walked up to it, put his big hands on it and pushed. It fell and broke, leaving a big hole in it. I was so upset; and then Nadine took Manar's birthday cake in its plastic cake dish and cover and put the entire dish upside down. Cute. What an exasperating day.

On October 1, Manar began walking and he never crawled again. He'd been taking steps since 9 and 10 months. But then on the 1st he just started walking from room to room and became even more of a disaster! He's so fast! So I guess weight has nothing to do with a baby walking or not (he's 36 pounds at 12 months).

In February 1982, Abu Nouman came to visit us. We looked forward to this as he loved his grandchildren and was a delight to have around the house. He would often go to the office with Maher during the day, which invoked a sense of pride for both of them.

The children both had minor colds and already I had to deal with Manar's high fever, which thankfully remained under 104 degrees. Nadine was getting sicker and it concerned me, since it seemed different than her usual illness. She had a nonstop fever that was rising alarmingly fast. The second day of Abu Nouman's arrival, Nadine's fever reached 106 degrees. She was burning up.

Abu Nouman with Manar

I had to act quickly or felt I would lose her. I stripped her down and put her in front of the air conditioner, hoping to cool her down. Abu Nouman objected to what I was doing and told me to wrap her instead. I told Maher to keep his father away from me and Nadine and that I knew what I had to do. I ran upstairs with Nadine. I was convinced that I was doing the right thing, but I was afraid Abu Nouman would talk to Maher and prevail. I was sure Nadine would die if wrapped up in a blanket.

I must have been very compelling, as neither man encroached on my actions. The air conditioning helped slightly, but not enough. I ran a bath with ice cubes and put her in it. This brought her temperature down and I felt better. The next 24 to 48 hours were hell. Nadine's fever would spike and I would artificially cool her down again. I also worried that Maher and his father would change their mind and try to take Nadine away from me. Finally, on the third day, the fever passed. I was certain she had malaria.

I had never experienced such fright as I did that week, except for Nadine's choking bout on the airplane after she was born. But this time it had happened to me in my own home. It made me think again of the health care system in the Middle East and the cultural differences in treating sick children.

Just as Nadine was getting better, another amazing occurrence happened that no one could have predicted. It rained in Sharjah! We had never seen it rain here in the Gulf. No one could remember the last time it had rained. It didn't just rain, it poured

— for 36 nonstop hours. At first it was weird, then it was neat and then it was horrible because it didn't stop. The water had no place to go. The Gulf was not set up with drains for this much rain and the sand was too hard to be absorbent. We watched as the water rose and filled our gated yard with a foot of black sewage.

We were lucky that the house was built much higher than the yard. By the time the rain stopped, it was up to the top step, just below the porch. Maher and Abu Nouman wore high, dark green rubber boots to get from the gate to the house. I don't know where they got those boots and I didn't ask. It was quite a sight to watch them dredge through the black water to the front marble deck. They

Too much rain

brought a pump from the factory and it took three days to pump out the water.

The servant's quarters in the back were flooded since it was ground level with the rest of the yard. Vicky, our helper from the

Philippines whom we had on a two-year contract, moved in with us. She loved the children and was wonderful. We worked on cleaning her little house up first and worried about the rest later.

My garden, trees included, was completely destroyed. Nothing survived except the original bougainvilleas on the gate and door. It was devastating as I looked around and saw nothing but black stuff on everything. I was grateful however that the house and all our possessions were spared. I would just have to start over again on my garden.

One evening in April 1982 was a landmark of sorts for me. I was having a dinner party and the guest of honor was a prince from Saudi Arabia. He had graduated from a university in New York and was Maher's company's sponsor in Saudi Arabia. The prince was kind and well-educated. I served leg of lamb as the main course along with the traditional *hummus*, *tabouleh*, *fatoush*, olives, *khubz* (Arabic bread) and so on. The prince was pleasantly surprised that I could cook Arabic food and enjoyed the meal. What was more important, however, was Maher's faith in me that I could cook for a prince, an Arab prince at that, and pull it off.

When everyone from the dinner party left except for one of our friends, we sat and talked for a while. It was the first and only time I heard such dangerous ideas expressed out in the open and in front of a woman. This man, unbeknownst to me, was of Palestinian descent. He talked of the struggle for his homeland and was quite angry. It was clear that he was very active and a part of the radical arm of Palestine that was fighting for their home-land. This made me very uncomfortable, but I was in my home and Maher was with me. Obviously Maher was aware of his friend's ideas. We were never political and stayed away from dis-cussing politics — at least I did. I never heard Maher discuss politics with anyone before.

I went to the *souk* (market) every other day not just because everything was fresh, but because the electrical supply was so sporadic things would spoil quickly, even in the refrigerator. With the extreme heat you could only keep what was needed for a day or two. The *souk* was covered with a large canopy of sorts to keep the sun out and the fruit and vegetables cool. The merchants dressed in their *dishdashes*, the traditional Arab dress, and wore either a white, or red and white, headpiece. The *fa wa ki* (fruit) smelled sweet and inviting: cantaloupe, watermelon, mangoes, bananas, nectarines, apples, grapes, cherries, strawberries, apricots, lemons and more. Vegetables were also on display: carrots, onions, dates, spinach, parsley, tomatoes, scallions, dill, lentils, eggplants, garlic, mint, black-eyed peas, chickpeas, squash, radishes, potatoes, endives, watercress, pinto beans, kidney beans, cabbages, peppers, cucumbers, artichoke hearts, black olives and beets. The merchants were experts at explaining how perfect their fruit was, which ones I should buy, and at what price.

I loved the anticipation of going, especially now that I had started to barter. I would take a deep breath and tell myself I could do it. I wanted to feel confident. I had watched and listened to Maher and his father bargain with them — it seemed like a sport. So I walked up to them smiling, speaking my best Arabic with authority as if I knew what the heck I was doing. Not bad — perhaps they took pity on me, but I do believe they too had fun. Each time I got a little better, which surprised the merchants, who did indeed enjoy sparring with me.

One day while negotiating for some ripe mangoes, two British women were also buying fruit. I watched out of the corner of my eye while the merchant took full advantage of them and charged them nearly four times what I had just paid. I smiled, looked knowingly into the eyes of the merchant (he somehow knew I would say nothing), and resumed my buying. "Learn the language, ladies," I thought to myself. I was, of course, at least in my own mind, the cat's meow at this point.

As time passed, I heard a few people describe me as *nos ou nos*, which means "half and half." Half American and half Arab. A smile would come to my face and to my heart…

Chapter Sixteen

It's Okay, Habeebe

I was lying in bed with Maher one night and he was very upset. Something was happening to his job and he didn't know what to do. Was Marblo going out of business? Though Maher got a lot of money from his father, he suggested we move to another villa, telling me everything would be fine. We moved in and furnished the villa just before my sister arrived for Christmas in 1982.

I was so excited that Debbie was coming for a visit. I had long awaited a visitor from my family — I had lived in the Middle East over seven and a half years now — and to have one of my sisters come meant the world to me. What struck me most the moment she arrived was that saying goodbye would be very difficult, and I would miss her very much.

Since this was a very special Christmas, I ordered a

Christmas with Debbie
was wonderful

Debbie with a camel

Christmas tree from Holland and had it flown in. It was big and gorgeous and came with a few extras I hadn't expected — a full complement of roots. It looked like Paul Bunyan had grabbed the trunk and simply plucked it out of the ground. The florist in Sharjah obviously had not been to the States for Christmas, nor did she understand what I wanted. So I placed the tree in a large bucket of water in the house, and we all decorated it. Wouldn't you know it, the darned Christmas tree soon began to grow. By the time we took it down, it had new growth on every branch, a sign that it was indeed a very special Christmas.

Christmas was a joy. Debbie brought wonderful gifts for the children, who absolutely adored her, and I gave her a pair of Turkish, gold intricate earrings.

We traveled to some of the other emirates so Debbie could get a flavor of the area — El Ain, Abu Dhabi and Dubai. There was much for her to see — camels, desert, the Sharjah *souk*, the Corniche of Abu Dhabi, the Clock Tower of Abu Dhabi, the blue, blue waters of the Arabian (Persian) Gulf, and of course, more desert. I know she had a very memorable time. And, yes, it was very difficult to say goodbye to Debbie. Not because I wanted to go back to Wisconsin with her, but because I knew my heart belonged here. This was my home, and I was very happy to stay with my little family.

Sisters share a goodbye hug

Maher left for Beirut in March 1983 and then traveled to Greece and Italy with his brother, Nouman. His trip would last at least two weeks. I was leery of this trip with his brother, though I wasn't sure why. Things were not good at work for Maher and I really had no idea what he was up to. The only thing he told me was that he was looking for different work.

The day Maher left was a disaster for Nadine and Manar. Both children cried their little hearts out, especially Nadine. She indeed was Daddy's little girl. He would take her to the office and she would sit on his lap and absolutely be in heaven. When I put her to bed she would tell me that Daddy was gone too long and would ask when he was coming home. Every night I explained that Daddy had lots of business in Beirut and Italy, all of which she understood since she had visited these countries. She stopped crying after a couple of nights and was now trying to explain it to Manar, who once in awhile would call out for Daddy and cringe his eyes as if about to cry. Nadine became a big help and would put her arm around him and say, "It's okay, *habeebe*" (Arabic word of endearment). "Daddy is in Beirut on business and he'll be back soon." It was so touching I could hardly stand it. How I loved them.

At the same time, my hives were getting out of control. As a young girl I helped my aunt one summer, shortly after she had delivered twins. She had two other young children as well, so I went to help for a couple of weeks. They had a strawberry patch. Since strawberries were one of my favorites I ate a lot of them during those two weeks, and broke out from head to toe with huge hives.

I'm certain that the stress of being alone in the Gulf with the children aggravated the hive problem that hadn't surfaced in years. I'm sure the heat didn't help either. I woke up one morning with huge hives from my neck down. I reasoned I had to cleanse my body of all the acid buildup from all the fruit I had been eating lately. I restricted my diet to only water and bread. It worked; the hives were gone after a week.

Nadine started preschool and loved it. Three languages were taught — French, Arabic and English. The schoolmistress was French and the school was called Les Bourgeon. Nadine's shyness was somewhat of a hindrance at first, but little by little she learned to open up in the classroom. She liked her teacher — that's what mattered.

Manar was very eager go to school with Nadine. Every morning when I dropped Nadine off, Manar insisted on

Nadine at school

standing in line with her as she waited to go to the classroom. Manar would give her a big hug and kiss and then wave goodbye as Nadine disappeared.

Manar finally began to talk when he was two and a half years old, but just a little. The only time he really said anything was when Nadine recited letters and words for him to repeat. He would say them perfectly for her. But boy, what a ham. He learned to say please, and when I'd get angry with him or tell him no, he would look up at me, smile with those eyes of his, and say a big please with a very heavy accent. I just melted and he knew it. What a darling little devil.

My little boy with the big smile

Chapter Seventeen

Password: Bernadette

The children and I arrived in the States on July 15, 1983. Conditions in the Gulf were no longer good for us as a family. Maher decided we should move to Appleton and live in the condo we purchased just before Nadine was born in 1978. Maher was looking for different job prospects in Saudi Arabia with his older brother, Nouman. So the children and I moved back by ourselves.

I kept busy with the children and Maher sent us money to live on. With the fighting escalating in the Middle East and Maher's job search, I had no idea how long we would stay in Appleton. At first I thought it would be a few short months. But then more months passed by, and there was little communication with Maher.

In May 1984, the children and I adjusted to Maher's

Nadine and Manar

Cousins

second long trip away from us. I really did not know what was going on with his work prospects and he didn't care to share. After all the months alone, the children settled in and seemed to be well adjusted to the new extended family of maternal grandparents, aunts, uncles and cousins, along with their new home and country. Getting to know their new grandparents was exciting, and their cousin, Beth, who was just three months older than Manar, became best friends with both of them. Beth was my sister Sue's daughter, and the three of them were inseparable.

Maher missed Christmas with us back in the States. He came in January 1985 and left again February 1. Maher and I began to drift apart because of the lengthy time away from each other. I never expected us to be apart this long and didn't understand what was happening in Saudi Arabia. He never shared any details about what was going on, even though I asked repeatedly.

Being apart from us seemed to change him. When he finally came back to the States to be with us, he was different — much different. I tried to ignore the changes, but he got irritated so easily. If I placed a decorative pillow in the wrong place, he would get upset. That was so unlike him. He never before had questioned anything so trivial around the home and had always deferred to my judgment. He also became very opinionated and criticized me for the littlest things. He didn't like the fact that I worked out at a gym and that I was becoming slightly muscular. And finally, he began giving me orders.

I didn't know, understand, or like this different man. It seemed Saudi Arabia and traveling with Nouman was having an adverse effect on him. Or was he simply under so much pressure he took out his frustration on those closest to him? When I asked him what was wrong, he always said everything was all right.

I was also concerned with our financial situation. Since Maher handled all the finances, I had no idea where we stood. Nothing was in my name — not even a credit card or bank account. Everything was paid for in cash when we lived in the Gulf. He wasn't working as far as I knew, but I assumed his father was giving him money.

Our ninth wedding anniversary had come and gone. Maher called just before Labor Day and said he would be coming to the States. He had business in Chicago on Labor Day and would fly to Appleton the next day. I thought it improbable for him to have business on Labor Day when nothing was open, so I told him it didn't make any sense, especially since he knew no one in Chicago. I had suspected things were probably going on when he traveled with his brother to Saudi Arabia, or wherever else he was traveling to. I asked him if he was having an affair. He denied everything and said he would see me soon.

It was very tense between us in Appleton. I just didn't believe him anymore. I didn't know what to believe. He had a locked briefcase that he always carried, and when he left the house one day I began to play with the combination. If I knew Maher, it would be something simple. I figured the combination out fairly quickly. Opening up the briefcase, I found several Polaroid pictures of a blonde woman that I didn't know.

When the children were sleeping, I confronted Maher with the pictures. He told me she was an English model — as though that made it a justifiable excuse. He said she meant nothing; I shouldn't let something like this get in the way of our marriage. I was furious, but asked him quietly and patiently if there were others. I didn't think he could help but brag. Apparently in his travels with his brother, much went on. I was so hurt and so angry I wanted to explode. I thought of Nadine and Manar sleeping and didn't want to wake them so I calmed down.

I couldn't wait for him to leave us. At that moment, I didn't

Family outing

care if I ever saw him again. I could remain married to him, I thought to myself, but he could go away and leave me alone, and that would be okay.

We celebrated the Fourth of July with my sister, Debbie, and her husband, Jeff, at their home on Lake Winnebago in Neenah. It was warm and sunny with a slight breeze — a perfect day for a picnic and celebration. They had a big party for friends and family. There was a huge pig roast, water-filled balloons for the children and adults, music and singing. Two of my friends, Bert and Toby, were there with their two small children. We engaged in some serious discussions about my return to the Middle East. We were singing along with some "oldies but goodies" playing on the radio when the subject of a password came up, a word or phrase to use if I found myself trapped or endangered when I returned to the Gulf. It had been almost a year since I confronted Maher about the other women, and though we weren't talking or seeing each other much, things seemed to be improving. Not a lot, but enough so that the people celebrating that day knew I would be returning because I was committed to my family. The song "Bernadette" came on, and I said, "Hey, that's my religious confirmation name!" Soon everyone was singing "Bernadette," and Bert and Toby said that should be my password — if ever I needed it.

How silly I thought, to have a password. But instinctively I knew I was uneasy about returning. I guess my family and friends were uneasy, too.

Chapter Eighteen

Folly of the Heart

In August 1985, Maher secured a new job in Abu Dhabi as general manager for an English publishing company opening up an office there. He knew I was reluctant to come back to him and reminded me that the women in his life before meant nothing. I shouldn't let the past ruin our marriage. He loved me and only me. He said we should all meet in Athens, Greece, for a week-long vacation before going back together to Abu Dhabi. It was time for us to be a family again. Besides, things in the Gulf were safer now.

Why would I go back? I was raised to believe that once married, you stayed with your husband. We had been married for over 10 years, many wonderful years, and it was those wonderful years that made me decide I had to go back. Not because I thought everything would be wonderful again, but because I knew how much my husband had loved me and the children and perhaps a spark of that remained. I didn't go back because I was sure things were going to work out. It was rather the opposite. I had to go back to make sure that if the marriage did fail that I had given it another chance. I wanted to make sure I had done all I could do before calling it quits. In my gut, I knew it was the wrong decision. In my heart, I still loved him.

Mom, Dad, and many family members took us to the airport in Appleton. We said our goodbyes with hugs and kisses and I walked outside to the airplane. Nadine and Manar were in front of me, and I knew I couldn't look back. Looking back would turn me into a pillar of salt, like Lot's wife, unable to continue my journey. The children turned around and waved, tempting me to catch another glimpse of the safety and love I was leaving behind. I prodded them forward, even as I fought the desire to turn back.

We got in the plane and the children sat down. I tried to sit, but instead was transfixed, standing with one hand on the seat to the left and one hand on the seat to the right. It was as though an outside power refused to let me sit. I bent over to look out the window, and there were the black silhouettes of my family. I thought about grabbing the children and running out of the plane. At that moment, however, I was asked to sit down as the plane started to taxi. In a trance, I sat down and knew it was too late. Getting on the plane was a mistake — I might not ever see my family again.

Though the children were sad to be leaving their extended family in the States, they were so happy to be seeing their father once again. It was a long flight, and I tried to raise my spirits for our arrival in Greece.

We landed and Maher was there to meet us. The children ran to him and put their arms around him. They were ecstatic to be with him. I knew, just by looking at him, that I had made a terrible mistake. His eyes, the reflection of his soul, were distant and empty. This was not the same man I married, and I knew that Maher and I could never be in love again. I no longer trusted him. I no longer felt the way I used to. I felt sad, like a weight had been tied around my heart and dropped — a weight that had gotten heavier over the last two years because of mistrust, deceit and separation.

We got into a taxi and went to our hotel in Athens where we had a two-room suite. It was lovely and the children got into their swimsuits to go down to the pool. As I lay next to my husband that night, I told him the children and I had to return to the States. It was a mistake for me to bring them here. I was sorry, but I needed to return. I was staring up at the ceiling, wondering how the words had escaped from my mouth. I was telling the truth, but I was surprised I said it so casually when I knew how much it would hurt him. Perhaps the last two years had finally pushed me beyond the point of caring anymore. They had changed me, and perhaps I wasn't the same person he had married either.

He pleaded with me, and for the second time in his life he cried so profoundly that my heart broke. Although he never apologized for his unfaithfulness, perhaps this was the best he could do. A small part of me wanted to believe he was genuinely sorry and could again be the man I knew and loved. I was so taken by this seemingly honest outburst of emotion that I told him I would continue on to Abu Dhabi. I told him it was okay — never mind what I said — I would go with him. This was my second mistake.

The week we spent in Greece was so wonderful for the children — to them we were a family again. Every day we went sightseeing at the ancient ruins, went shopping for clothes in downtown Athens, and went swimming back at the hotel. The children's joy made it even more unbearable for me. I could not fake my unhappiness, though I tried. Maher was pretending like nothing had happened, that we were once again a happy family, now reunited, and he was the hero. How long would it take for this fairy tale to come crashing down on the children? How long before they, too, discovered that he lived a secret life that did not include his wife or children. Yes, he claimed that his several affairs and outrageous lifestyle in Saudi Arabia meant nothing — I was his wife and nothing could change his love for me — but something had changed. He changed, and I sensed his love for me had changed as well.

He gave me a beautiful white and yellow gold bracelet in Athens. Was it his attempt to buy my love and my happiness? What I really needed was time to heal. What he needed was time to prove he could be the same man I married. I only felt one thing after our trip to Athens — time was running out.

Chapter Nineteen

The Darkness Grows

We arrived back to Abu Dhabi to settle in our new apartment. I was struck at how different things were for me this time. The city I grew to love was now unattractive. Life was no longer carefree; it was difficult. I felt overwhelmed by the smallest difficulties. Shortly after we arrived I was doing clothes in our new washing machine. Something happened, and every piece in the wash was ruined. Instead of taking it in stride, as I would have before, I was furious and started to cry. When I was happy, nothing kept me from tackling a problem or situation. I was not dismayed by the extreme heat and humidity. I made a game out of the trickling, running water. The rats and cockroaches, sporadic electricity, and air conditioning going out when it was over 100 degrees was part of daily life. But now, it was impossible to cope.

Maher noticed that I was not adjusting to him, or the Gulf, as I had in the past. He became very demanding and very impatient. He told me I had to cover myself in public now. I didn't have to wear a *chador*, but I did have to become more modest and start covering my legs. Why had this suddenly become an issue? Was this not the same country where I used to garden in my swimsuit? I was dismayed. Things were tense between us. I was not responding to him as before and he was upset with me. I told him he needed to give me time for everything to work out. But he had no patience and no time to give me. He couldn't understand why I was acting the way I was, and he wouldn't listen.

Nadine and Manar enrolled in the American School of Abu Dhabi. Manar had long outgrown his silent spell of speaking and was enjoying the other children and the learning. He could look at something just once and remembered everything about it, almost as if he had a photographic memory. He loved taking things apart and putting them together again. Nadine was enjoying the friends and subjects as well. It was a wonderful school — the best-equipped school I had ever seen — better even than those in the States. A large room with the latest computer equipment was available to all the students. The school was run by a highly-qualified American professor who had been in the Gulf nearly as long as I had.

One evening, Maher demanded that I act as I had before, at least in the bedroom. I should forget everything and be the wife he remembered. How could he ask such a thing? How could he so easily separate our intimacy at night from what happened the rest of the day? I refused at first, but then I got angry and made love to him as an act of vengeance. When he realized what I was doing, he grabbed me by both wrists and pushed me aside. He did not appreciate my little stunt, and for the first time, he struck me. I didn't know what to do. It was obvious that I was now dealing with a different man, a stranger. I was now back in a third-world country that did not recognize the rights of women. I was in trouble.

I also knew that to tell anyone, even my best girlfriend, Adla, would be impossible. She would be required by Muslim law to tell her husband. If she knew something and didn't tell her husband, she would be at fault. I couldn't take the risk. I could not share with any Arab what was happening or what I was thinking.

A week later, when the children were asleep, Maher and I had an argument about signing a document written in Arabic (I spoke Arabic but could not read it). We were in the living room. He told me the signed document would turn over our condo in Appleton to him as the sole owner. I refused to sign. He beat me, leaving bruises on my wrists and my neck. He pulled clumps of hair out of my head. I was down on the floor, sobbing. I tried to be quiet so as not to waken the children, and I begged him to be quiet, too. He didn't seem to care. I had never seen him so angry. I was terrified, but I did not sign the document.

The next day after dropping the children off at school, I wrote a letter to my mom and dad telling them if I ever signed a document giving Maher sole ownership of the condo that it was signed under duress. I asked them to please forward this letter to my attorney. I asked the school office to mail my letter so that no one else, especially Maher, would be suspicious. If there was ever another fight, I might have to sign it — it was not worth my life.

Maher became increasingly paranoid that I might try to return to the States because he knew I was so unhappy. He had his employees watch me. I suspected the phone was tapped at home, and if I wanted to go anywhere, he required a driver to take me. The only safe haven was the American School of Abu Dhabi. I decided I needed to meet and speak with Dr. Jones (not his real name), the American professor, because I needed someone to confide in and perhaps ask for help.

I was always fine as long as the children were awake, but I dreaded the evenings. And then came the night that would change my life forever — Maher was drinking. He again wanted me to sign the document. This time he would not take no for an answer. I tried to resist but again he beat me — this time more severely than before. I was strong and in shape, but I felt like a rag doll. I could not believe that I could be so easily beaten. He told me that if I did not sign, he would get rid of me — I would be taken to the desert and never be seen again. (It wasn't uncommon for people to be buried up to the neck in the desert with a box placed over their head, left to die a horrible death in the hot desert sun.) Then he made a phone call, his back turned to me, asking someone to do this. It seemed real, but I wondered if he had pushed the button down on the receiver and was just being dramatic. I took it seriously. He was so worked up. He looked like a madman.

I was bent over on the carpet next to the couch, rocking myself. Tears ran down my cheeks. I put my hand over my mouth as I watched him come at me again, this time with a knife in his hand. All of a sudden, he grabbed his chest and fell next to me. I quickly moved away. I thought he was having a heart attack. He just laid there, and I knew he could do nothing to me now. I said to myself, "Please die." I grabbed the knife, knowing I should use it to save my life. Self defense. But I could not do it. I just stood and watched him. He recovered a few minutes later. I dropped the knife.

Enough was enough. I signed the document. I knew that

in order for me to survive I needed a different strategy. I needed to become someone else. I could not survive another beating. I also realized that if I had killed or injured my husband, I would have disappeared in a prison in the desert and no one in the world would have ever known what happened to me — not even my children.

Chapter Twenty

Mask of Safety

I became a new person in September 1985. I became very obedient. It pleased Maher. I could see him change and be nice again. It was a good beginning. I needed him to trust me again, which meant I had to act like he wanted me to act. He was still convinced that I would try to go back to the States. He told me that the children and I would never return to the States — ever.

I never contested him and always did what I was told. He was always testing me with his words, looking for a reaction— anything at all that showed him I was still defiant. He never saw it. I was completely subservient.

I started thinking about what I needed to do to get out of this situation alive. We belonged to a club at one of the nicest hotels in Abu Dhabi. It had a large, lovely pool and workout room. I knew from the beatings I needed to be stronger physically, so I started working out. We went every weekend.

Next, I decided I needed to see Dr. Jones. I met with him and told him everything. I told him that I needed his help in getting out of the country, that my husband was an Arab but not of local royalty, that I would not leave without my children, and that my husband had our passports in a large safe in his office. Dr. Jones agreed to take me to see the American consulate at the American Embassy. It was fairly close to the school, and we could walk in the desert (out the back door of the school) without anyone knowing — if, in fact, Maher had people watching again in front of the school.

We walked up to the gate of the embassy and were let in. We met with a new consulate who had just arrived in the country three weeks earlier, not the woman who had helped me get out of the Abu Dhabi prison. I was sitting in a chair on the left and Dr. Jones was on the right. I briefly told the consulate my story and he said, "Well, I just can't believe that women have no rights here." I leaned back in my chair, turned to Dr. Jones and said, "I'm never going to get out of here, am I?" Dr. Jones asked him if he could issue new passports for the children and me. He said yes. I said, "Of course, the visas need to be in there that we legally entered the country." That he couldn't do. "But without the visas, the passports are useless," I said. After pleading with him a few more minutes, Dr. Jones told him to please issue new passports, and we left.

Once outside, Dr. Jones said, "The man is new and he obviously knows nothing about this country." We walked slowly and silently through the desert, back to the school. My mind was racing as to what I would have to do now. Somehow I needed to get my hands on the original passports. If that meant blowing up the safe, then that's what I was going to have to do.

I was so good at this new act of mine that I began to receive beautiful long-stemmed red roses from Maher — every week. I knew that I was beginning to win his trust. Then a break came.

Maher returned home one evening and said he had to take a trip to India. This was the first time since I returned that he was leaving on a business trip; he was still suspicious I would flee if he left me for even a short time.

I didn't skip a beat. I told him the children and I would miss him, then went on my merry way doing household chores.

He was leaving the next morning. However, something didn't feel right. I squelched my inclination to call Dr. Jones the moment I was alone. I began to think this was a test and that I would be closely monitored. I listened to my gut instinct and did nothing to leave.

The next day, he informed me that the trip was cancelled. He was watching me for a reaction, a slip of emotion. "Okay," I replied nonchalantly, surprised at how well I was acting. He returned to the office, and I sat down to think things through carefully. This was a test. I had passed it. Now I had to devise a plan.

I knew the only way I could ever get out of the country was to be well prepared. First, I had to get my hands on our original three passports. Second, I needed Dr. Jones to contact my family in the States and purchase one-way tickets for us. Third, Maher would have to be in the air traveling to another country for us to escape undetected. We would have to leave in the middle of the night to give us at least a 24-hour head start.

Leaving, however, was only the first part of the mission. It would get us only as far as the Abu Dhabi Airport — nothing more.

I arranged another meeting with Dr. Jones at the school. We were standing side by side outside the school, just looking out over the grounds. The parents had all dropped off their children. Since no one else was allowed inside the gates of the school, we were alone. He spoke as he looked straight ahead. "I'll help, but only if you promise me something." "Anything," I said. "I'll only help if you promise never to return." Of course I would never return — was there something else he wasn't saying? "No," he said flatly. "You don't understand. I will never again help anyone else if you return. I've seen it time and time again. The women always come back. Either the men beg them to come back and promise them the world, or they just can't make it on their own. So they come back for the money." God, no, I thought to myself. I couldn't imagine how any woman could return once she escaped. I turned to him and he turned to me. I looked him square in the eye and promised, "You will never, ever, see me again."

Manar's birthday

October 21, 1985, was Manar's fifth birthday. We had a big party for him at the hotel at which we were members. The party was at the pool area with a large table at the side of the pool for the food, cake and ice cream. The pool area was very large with outdoor games like foosball nearby. All of Manar's and Nadine's friends were there from school.

I was in the water playing with the children, tossing the large plastic beach ball. I got out to dry myself on the opposite side of the pool from where Maher was standing. He was next to the party table and casually bent down to pick up my purse.

I knew better than to keep anything written in the house. Maher would periodically go through all my drawers, closets and jewelry. The only thing I never saw him search before was my purse — until that day. I stopped breathing.

I knew I had to get away

I knew I couldn't go over and grab my purse — that would give me away and destroy any dreams I had of escaping. So I stood there and let him riffle through my purse, still unconsciously holding my breath. He seemed to be going through it so thoroughly that I was certain he would find the very small piece of folded, white paper hidden in my wallet — the piece of paper containing a flight number. I had been arranging flight information through Dr. Jones. He finally put the purse down, finding nothing, and went to get a drink. I began to breathe again.

Chapter Twenty-One

Ready to Run

Two months had passed since I had started planning to escape. On November 16, 1985, Maher came home after work and announced he had to go to India on a business trip. This time it felt right, like he was telling the truth. It had to be — I was going to put my life on the line because of that feeling. I knew if I got caught, I would disappear. My children would be returned to Maher without a mother. No one would ever know what happened to me.

I was glad I didn't have domestic help at our new apartment — it would have made things very complicated.

This time there was no advance notice of this trip. Maher's flight left that evening. It was late and the children were in their pajamas. Maher hugged and kissed them and said goodbye. I had never believed in angels before, but I did in the very next moment. Maher walked to the kitchen, and I heard the keys he always carried (I had no keys) drop on the countertop. Oh my . . . he trusted me enough to leave the keys. I needed those keys desperately. The keys to the office gave me access to our passports. He walked over to me, kissed me, and left.

I waited only 10 minutes after hearing Maher's driver pick him up and leave before returning to the children. "Guess what?" I said. "We're going to America!" They began jumping up and down with excitement on the living room couch where they had been sitting. I gave them each one suitcase, and told them to go to their rooms and pack. I was frantic to make the necessary phone calls and hoped my phone was clean now, that the phone taps had been removed. I had no other phone. My hope was that he was now completely convinced that I loved him and would never leave him. I put that theory to the test as I dialed my first number.

Dr. Jones answered and confirmed he had what I needed. Airline tickets to the States via England had been purchased with money from my family. I knew I needed to be on an English-speaking airline, and even though England was risky because the Tarabishi family had connections there and knew many other Arabs, it was my only choice. So British Airways it was. I ran to my bedroom and packed only what I could carry in my suitcase.

I looked around as if to say goodbye for the last time and noticed that Maher had left a wrapped box containing my birthday present, which was in ten days. I guess he wanted me to know that he had gotten me a gift to open when he returned. I believe it was a Rolex watch. I left it at the table and never touched it.

Before leaving, I grabbed a small piece of paper and pen to write a note to Maher. I left it on a small table next to his chair.

On top of the folded note I left my wedding band. The note said simply: "You should have never beaten me."

While Dr. Jones had our new passports (I had given them to him for safe keeping), I knew they were worthless without the visa stamps on the inside pages showing we arrived legally into the country. Without them, I would be pulled aside and my husband contacted (or his office, in his absence). I also had to make sure the taxi driver was not an Arab, but rather an Indian or Pakistani, because Muslim Arabs were required to turn in disloyal wives to their Muslim husbands. After flagging several taxis, I was finally able to get a Pakistani driver. I instructed him to drive me to Maher's office and asked him to wait.

Nadine and Manar came with me to the office door. Since I had the keys to the office, getting in wasn't a problem. It was late, after midnight, and the children were tired. I walked over to the enormous safe and stood paralyzed as soon as I saw the locking mechanism. I had gambled my life thinking it was a combination safe, something I could open rather quickly, like the lock on Maher's briefcase I had opened to discover pictures of the English model. I knew him well enough to know that the combination would be something easy to remember, like his birthday, our anniversary, or one of his children's birthdays. I hadn't really given it a second thought.

The safe had two round combination circles with levers. I had no idea how to open it. I was on my knees, just staring at it, watching my future and that of my children disappear into mechanical nothingness. Two locks. Two measly locks. How could I have been so stupid? The slideshow of my life started going through my head: Sharjah. Apartment. Children. Maher. Beatings. Nightfall. More Beatings. Tears. Silence. Children. Beatings. Buried. Desert. Box over my head. Children.

Two locks. Think of something. Think of something. There was no other way. We needed those stamped visas on the passport. Then my mind started playing a very different slideshow, something more hopeful, as I looked around the office. Manar. Office. Trips with Maher. Safe? Locks?

I remembered Manar going to the office with Maher. Was it possible he had seen him open the safe? Is that something he would have noticed or watched? I looked to Manar standing on my right, my little engineer as I called him, because he loved to take apart whatever he could get his hands on and put it back together again. "Manar, have you ever seen Daddy open up the safe?" "Sure, Mom," he said. "Once." I knew once was enough for Manar. He could duplicate anything he saw. I moved over and said to my five-year-old, "Honey, open the safe for Momma." "Sure, Mom."

I watched him carefully work the dials. Though I was very calm, I was scared to death. "It's open, Mom," he said. He stepped away. I pulled the large, heavy door open and there they were: our three passports sitting right on top in the middle of the safe. There was a huge pile of cash beneath them.

Passports

Carefully, without touching a single *dirham* or dollar, I lifted the three passports out. They were like gold to me. I cradled them against my chest with one hand and closed the safe with the other.

Once back inside the taxi, I told the driver the address to Dr. Jones's house. Again the driver waited for my return. Dr. Jones was up and waiting for us. He couldn't believe I had the original passports. He handed over our tickets, we hugged, then said our goodbyes. I looked into his eyes and he knew it meant I would never see him again. He could tell. He smiled, and wished me luck.

The airport was more than an hour in the desert. Once there I knew we would have a long wait, but I needed to do this in the dead of the night so no one would see us. The children were so very tired. I had six dollars in my purse, my children, one suitcase for each of us, and my jewelry, in case I needed to sell it. It was enough. It had to be.

Chapter Twenty-Two

Four Checkpoints

We arrived at the airport, and I knew I had at least four checkpoints to go through without my husband. This was a very unusual event in the Gulf. An Arab husband or adult male member of the family almost always accompanied his wife and children, especially when traveling. I was betting that even though it was obvious I was a blonde, blue-eyed American woman with her two Arab-looking children that I could skillfully use my Arabic and yes, my charm, to get through the checkpoints. If I didn't, there would be no second chances.

I saw a black phone on the table as I neared the first check-point. I knew I must do and say exactly the right thing. If they got suspicious, they would call Maher to make sure it was okay that I was traveling to the States alone, and with his children.

I had to put my nerves aside and relax. I shyly smiled, saying *"Marhaba"* (Hello) as I handed over the three passports to the first guard. They were dressed like military guards, one standing behind the other. He seemed nice, and I could tell he was pleased that I addressed him in Arabic. That was good. He looked at my children and said they were Arab. "Yes," I said enthusiastically with a big smile. "Aren't they beautiful?" He agreed. I said we were just on a small visit to the States while their father was so busy with business. He nodded as if to understand. I reached out my hand for the passports with a cheery smile once more and he handed them back to me. *"Shoo kran ik teer"* (Thank you very much) I said, and again he was delighted.

I hoped I would be as lucky at the next checkpoint.

I repeated the same routine for the second checkpoint. Then the third. It's a good thing I'm a woman, I thought as we cleared checkpoint three. Men can be gullible. The stress was making me a bit giddy.

We were getting closer, I knew, but the real test would be at the fourth checkpoint. It was there we'd have to wait out the night until our plane left. I would know by then if someone had seen us leave.

We passed through the fourth checkpoint and sat at the gate, waiting for our plane. I chose a line of chairs against the wall so I could see those around me or approaching me from any direction. We had a long wait. The children slept on either side of me. I thought this would be the easy part — waiting. In many ways it was the most difficult, and most nerve-wracking. Up to this point I had been an active participant, deciding how I would act and carry out what needed to be done. But here, waiting, there was little I could do. Maher would discover that I had left, or he wouldn't. There was nothing I could do about that now. And so I sat. And watched. I smiled shyly if anyone came near — one way to cover up my stress. Thankfully there were not many travelers at this time of night.

The waiting continued. Each look at the clock started the slideshow in my mind of getting caught and buried and killed. Finally it was time to board, and I woke the children to get in line.

We were in our seats on the British Airways airplane. As soon as the plane was in the air, I wrote a note and pushed the button for service. The stewardess came to me, and I asked her to give the folded note to the pilot. The note stated that I was an American citizen fleeing my abusive Arab husband. She returned and asked that I follow her — the pilot wished to speak to me personally. I left my sleeping children and followed her to the cockpit. The captain turned around, shook my hand, and looked me in the eye. "I have only one question to ask," he said. "Is your husband of Arab royalty?" I would have lied but was thankful I didn't have to. I answered, "No, he comes from a wealthy family but he is not of Arab royalty." "Good, then we'll call ahead and make sure you are taken to a safe area while you wait for your connecting flight to Chicago. And oh, Miss . . . good luck to you."

The first leg of the trip was going as planned. Or so I thought. Ever vigilant, we were escorted to a large room after landing in London and remained there alone for several hours. I was so grateful — I did not want to have to watch with suspicion every dark-skinned Arab male who came close to me. It was such a long, agonizing wait. Every set of footsteps outside the door reminded me that someone could still come into the room to harm us or take us back. With my husband's money and connections, especially in London, it was not out of the question. By now he could have certainly called home to check in, just to make sure I was still there.

At least waiting in this room, for the moment safe with my children, was much better than being outside. The children slept; I watched the door.

We boarded our next flight non-stop to O'Hare Airport in Chicago. It was a 747, and it was close to being full of passengers. The flight was uneventful, and I was beginning to think that perhaps we could actually make it to the States before being discovered missing from Abu Dhabi. We still had a long way to go.

We deplaned in Chicago and walked to the customs area. I was carrying three suitcases and trying to keep Nadine and Manar close to me. The children would be easy targets at this point, even though we were three people among hundreds. I scanned the area and it was then that I saw them. Three dark-haired, dark-skinned men were approaching me quickly, directly ahead. The one in the middle was flanked by one on his right and one on his left. They were dressed in dark clothes. I stopped in my tracks, and without hesitation they walked right up to me. "Mrs. Tarabishi?"

Dear God, I thought to myself, they got me — we almost made it. I wondered if I would have an opportunity to use my password — if I could somehow get word back to my family that I made it this far. I felt my shoulders slump and my whole body cave in. I don't know how I continued to stand. I said simply, "Yes."

The man in the middle drew out his badge and said, "Ma'am, we're with the Chicago Police Department and we're here to protect you."

Shock. Disbelief. Joy. How my heart withstood that information is still beyond me. I stood straight, took a breath, and put my heart back in my body.

They escorted us out of the airport and into a police car, and we drove to a nearby building on airport property. I asked how in the world they knew we were arriving, or for that matter, how they knew anything about us. I had never called them.

My sister, Sue, and family had talked with the State Department and the police in Chicago. They had also arranged for my safety in London. All this time I was thinking I was alone. This was my fight, and no one elses. I guess my parents and siblings didn't agree. Without my knowing, they had made it their fight, too. They had shared in my anxiety and fear each step of the way, had waited for the confirmations, had probably doubted their decisions to intervene out of love. Tears welled up inside me. Fighting alone, the world and circumstances could be terrible and overwhelming. But in the midst of love, the world suddenly became a smaller, more hopeful place.

The police brought us to another private room, away from everyone else until it was time for our final flight. I could still hear the footsteps outside the door, but I wasn't quite as frightened anymore. And when those footsteps opened the door, it was to make sure we were okay and to offer us something to drink.

When it was time to catch our flight to Appleton, the police personally escorted us. I remembered walking down the long corridor to the gate, with all the other passengers and travelers looking at us. I expected the police to leave us there, but they boarded the plane, motioning for us to follow. This was done before anyone else had a chance to board. They checked out the plane thoroughly before departing. I thanked them profusely, sat down, and was afraid to think any further. It was indeed good to be back in America.

As we took off, I knew it was still possible for Maher and his family to have a private jet flown into little Outagamie Airport and whisk us off the minute our plane touched down.

They had the money, and Maher still knew people in this area from his college days in Milwaukee. He had also spent time in Chicago on business, and I had seen what Maher could do when he was desperate.

I was vigilant as we landed. The plane came to a stop. I looked out the window toward the airport and saw the silhouettes of my entire family pressed against the window. It was dark with a small smattering of snow on the ground. I let most of the other passengers off first. We would be slow moving. We walked down the stairs onto the tarmac.

It seemed a very long distance to the outside door of the small terminal where my family was waiting. I looked to the right and then to the left. I saw no other planes. I saw no one else but passengers. I took a deep breath of cold air and walked slowly with Nadine and Manar close to me, then a little faster. I saw my family leave the window and run to the door to meet us.

We walked into the arms of my crying, deliriously happy family.

We had made it.

I was home again.

Chapter Twenty-Three

The Day After

I knew I would have to confront Maher soon, in some way. He would act quickly. I knew how easily money and influence could stretch a long hand from the Middle East to far away places like Neenah. Maher would contact me, or his "associates" would make an attempt to either kidnap the children or kill me. Even in safety I was a realist. I had been married to this man for ten and a half years and had seen him at his worst. (I learned many years later that my dad was a realist, too. When I left the security of their home a month later to live in our house in Appleton, unbeknownst to me, he made nightly round trips and sat in my driveway keeping vigil for about a month, patiently greeting each dawn, just to make sure his daughter and grandchildren were safe.)

The phone rang the next day at my parent's home, where

the children and I were staying for the time being. It was Maher — he wanted to speak with me. I was upstairs, and I took the call in the hallway where I could have some privacy. Everyone else was downstairs, and I was grateful for that.

Maher begged me to come home. He would never hit me again, ever. He would give me a separate bank account with as much money in it as I wanted. Promise followed promise, until my heart stopped listening and spoke through the clamor. "No."

He cried. I cried. I had said it, but did I really mean it? The doubts returned. I was beginning to weaken. It would be so much easier to go back. Maybe it took me running away for him to finally see his mistakes and change. Was there a chance, even an outside chance, that I could have the loving family back I had dreamed of? Probably not, but maybe it would be close. I loved him so much — could I love him enough to change him for good? And then I remembered Dr. Jones's words — "I will help you only if you promise never to come back." I shook my head. I had to stick to my promise — I had to. Yet I found my husband's words, his pressure, his wish to be together again as I had wished from the day we were married — commanding. I struggled between reality and hope, good versus evil, selfish desires and unselfish good. Is it right to suddenly stop loving, to suddenly stop trying, to simply give up? Is that how I was raised? Was it not just one life, but four lives hanging in the balance? I wavered, then made my decision.

"No."

I hung up. My knees gave out and I fell to the floor.

A SCENE FROM ABU DHABI CORNISH   U. A. E.

32 Feb. 87

Dearest Nadine —

Big Big and Long Kisses —

How are you and Manar — I am writing from ABOO DHABI at daddy office — Soon I will Visit U.S.A. and HOPE to see you. Regards to mummy. Love your grand Pa. Jeddo Moh. A. TARABICHI

TO Miss. Nadine Tarabichi

ADDRESS

CITY APPLETON

STATE WIS. 54915

U. S. A.

FIS/PC/307

Epilogue

I wonder if I would have been strong enough if Dr. Jones had not made me promise never to come back — that he would never help another woman if I returned. It was an enormous responsibility for me to bear. There were women before me that needed his help, and I knew there would be women after me. I kept hearing his voice over and over again.

If you are still out there Dr. Jones, I thank you profoundly. I kept my promise. And I hope you were able to help others. You and my children are what got me out. I could not allow my daughter to be raised in a culture where it was acceptable for women to be physically and verbally abused. I could not allow my son to grow up in a culture that condoned treating women like that. Perhaps it is different there today. And perhaps we are not as advanced as we would like to think even in the United States, where women still struggle behind closed doors and closed curtains in abusive situations. But wherever we are, we must continue to work for what is right, and good, and loving in our relationships. Dr. Jones, my children gave me the strength to leave, and you reinforced it. No matter what, we were going to be free. And because of your help, we are still free today.

The calls from Maher and his family did not end after our return to the States. Like me, Maher and his parents still loved the children and wanted to see them. And though I couldn't live with how Maher treated me, I didn't hate him. I was wary, however, of his attempts to see the children, and refused time and time again.

A few years after our arrival in the States, Maher's oldest sister, Nadia, contacted me. She lived in Beverly Hills, California, and said her parents were arriving in a few weeks to visit her. Would it be possible for me and the children to join them in California? Abu Nouman and Umm Nouman wanted very much to see their grandchildren. All our expenses would be paid.

I thought about this briefly, long enough for the terrible thoughts to start going through my mind. I told her I would call her back after I had some time to think.

Of course, I thought of the distinct possibility that my children could be taken away from me — there had already been kidnapping attempts by Maher, so the threat was very real. Then I thought of how much Umm Nouman and Abu Nouman must have missed their grandchildren. This wasn't their fault. Do I deny them the right to see their own flesh and blood, whom they loved? I couldn't help but feel that they needed to see them. It would tear me apart, but I also knew it was important for my children to meet their grandparents again.

I called Nadia back after a couple of days and said we would come. She sent the tickets, and we were on our way.

As soon as I met with Umm Nouman and Abu Nouman, I knew I had made the right decision. They were in love with Nadine and Manar, head over heels all over again, when they laid eyes on them. They could do little more than sit and stare at the children, sharing their praises. How beautiful. How handsome. How well-behaved. How intelligent.

Eventually they asked me what happened and why I left Maher. Now it was my turn to stare. He had never told them. I figured he had shared something horrible about me, but nothing? Didn't he talk to his parents anymore? I told them in one sentence what he had done. They stared again, this time at me. Why didn't I call them? They would have fixed everything. They would not have tolerated Maher treating me in such a way — it was not acceptable. Maher still loved me. He has never loved another woman like he loved me. Come back with us and we will work everything out.

Did they hear what they were saying? And did they actually believe it, or had Maher put them up to this? They knew it would not have been right for me to call them behind Maher's back. I was so stunned I couldn't think. Did they really think this could happen? Besides, Maher had taken another wife before I even divorced him — how could this possibly work with two wives and the two new children from Maher's current relationship?

I simply shook my head. "No." I said it as softly and respectfully as I could because I loved them both. And I believed that beyond the divides of culture, and time, and love for their son, they still loved me. But even love seemed to carry with it boundaries, and those boundaries were filled with pain, a pain we shared.

We were driven back to the hotel on Rodeo Drive and I put the children to sleep. I sat in the dark, well into the night. When I had escaped and walked off the plane with my children into the arms of my family, I thought my relationships to the Middle East had ended. For good. But I realized then that my decision to leave was only one part of the relationship. Umm Nouman and Abu Nouman had never stopped loving me and they had never stopped loving their grandchildren. Perhaps Maher still loved me, and in a strange way, in a small corner of my heart, in a box that would never be opened again, perhaps there remained a love for Maher. Perhaps that is what made it so painful. Love's tentacles are not severed easily or cleanly.

In many ways, the story after our arrival back to the States was even more extraordinary than how we got there. A single mother with two children returning to a country I had not worked in for over ten years and six dollars in my pocket. The journey was difficult yet extremely rewarding.

The Arab world was one of fascination, intrigue and complication. The people are passionate, deeply devoted to their families and just as worried about their futures as we are. As much as I was committed to the prospect of spending the rest of my life in the Middle East, life happens and it changes our plans and we move forward.

If not confronted with this past history, I might never have learned what I was capable of accomplishing. I learned that I could determine what my life could be; that I could give form to my future; that I could protect my children with my tenacious determination and strong will. I began to trust in myself though doubt was never far behind — I would not let it win. I learned that the journeys we take could be triumphant. I learned that family is everything.

Nadine and Manar have grown to be amazing young adults; and I did finally remarry in 1999 to an exceptional man.

You absolutely can do what needs to be done to make your life healthy and whole in your relationships — either with family or with friends. It must be good and respectful — and you will know what that feels like when you follow your true self. Then your story of personal triumph will shine. — Nancy T. Wall, 2009